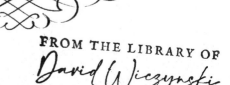

ISBN 978-1-334-49084-2
PIBN 10621589

1 MONTH OF
FREE
READING

at
www.ForgottenBooks.com

By purchasing this book you are eligible for one month membership to ForgottenBooks.com, giving you unlimited access to our entire collection of over 700,000 titles via our web site and mobile apps.

To claim your free month visit:
www.forgottenbooks.com/free621589

English
Français
Deutsche
Italiano
Español
Português

www.forgottenbooks.com

Mythology Photography **Fiction**
Fishing Christianity **Art** Cooking
Essays Buddhism Freemasonry
Medicine **Biology** Music **Ancient**
Egypt Evolution Carpentry Physics
Dance Geology **Mathematics** Fitness
Shakespeare **Folklore** Yoga Marketing
Confidence Immortality Biographies
Poetry **Psychology** Witchcraft
Electronics Chemistry History **Law**
Accounting **Philosophy** Anthropology
Alchemy Drama Quantum Mechanics
Atheism Sexual Health **Ancient History**
Entrepreneurship Languages Sport
Paleontology Needlework Islam
Metaphysics Investment Archaeology
Parenting Statistics Criminology
Motivational

Dramatic Literature

CYRANO DE BERGERAC. A Play in Five Acts. By EDMOND ROSTAND. Translated from the French by GLADYS THOMAS and MARY F. GUILLEMARD. Small 4to, 5s. Also, Popular Edition, 16mo, cloth, 2s. 6d. ; paper, 1s. 6d.

THE PLAYS OF W. E. HENLEY AND R. L. STEVENSON. Crown 8vo, cloth. An Edition of 250 copies only, 10s. 6d. net, or separately, 16mo, cloth, 2s. 6d. each, or paper, 1s. 6d.

DEACON BRODIE	ADMIRAL GUINEA
BEAU AUSTIN	MACAIRE

THE PLAYS OF ARTHUR W. PINERO. Paper covers, 1s. 6d. ; or cloth, 2s. 6d. each.

THE TIMES	THE AMAZONS
THE PROFLIGATE	THE NOTORIOUS MRS.
THE CABINET MINISTER	EBBSMITH
THE HOBBY HORSE	THE BENEFIT OF THE
LADY BOUNTIFUL	DOUBT
THE MAGISTRATE	THE PRINCESS AND THE
DANDY DICK	BUTTERFLY
SWEET LAVENDER	TRELAWNY OF THE
THE SCHOOL-MISTRESS	"WELLS"
THE WEAKER SEX	THE GAY LORD QUEX

* THE SECOND MRS. TANQUERAY

* This play can be had in Library form, 4to, cloth. With a Portrait of the Author, 5s.

THE PLAYS OF GERHART HAUPTMANN.

THE SUNKEN BELL. Fcap. 8vo, boards, 4s. net.

HANNELE. Small 4to, with Portrait, 5s. Paper covers, 1s. 6d. ; or cloth, 2s. 6d.

LONELY LIVES. Paper covers, 1s. 6d. : or cloth, 2s. 6d.

THE WEAVERS. Paper covers, 1s. 6d. ; or cloth, 2s. 6d.

CARLYON SAHIB. A Drama in Four Acts. By GILBERT MURRAY. Cloth, 2s. 6d. ; paper, 1s. 6d.

*

Dramatic Literature—*continued*

ANDROMACHE. A Play in Three Acts. By GILBERT MURRAY. Cloth, 2s. 6d. ; paper, 1s. 6d.

THE PRINCESS MALEINE: A Drama in Five Acts (Translated by GERARD HARRY), and THE INTRUDER: A Drama in One Act. By MAURICE MAETERLINCK. With an Introduction by HALL CAINE, and a Portrait of the Author. Small 4to, cloth, 5s. Paper covers, 1s. 6d.

THE FRUITS OF ENLIGHTENMENT: A Comedy in Four Acts. By Count LYOF TOLSTOY. Translated from the Russian by E. J. DILLON. With Introduction by A. W. PINERO. Small 4to, with Portrait, 5s. Paper covers, 1s. 6d.

THE GHETTO. A Drama in Four Acts. Freely adapted from the Dutch of Herman Heijermans, Jun., by CHESTER BAILEY FERNALD. 16mo, cloth, 2s. 6d.; paper, 1s. 6d.

KING ERIK: A Tragedy by EDMUND GOSSE. A Re-issue, with a Critical Introduction by Mr. THEODORE WATTS. Fcap. 8vo, boards, 5s. net.

THE PIPER OF HAMELIN: A Fantastic Opera in Two Acts. By ROBERT BUCHANAN. With Illustrations by HUGH THOMSON. 4to, cloth, 2s. 6d. net.

HYPATIA. A Play in Four Acts. Founded on CHARLES KINGSLEY's Novel. By G. STUART OGILVIE. With Frontispiece by J. D. BATTEN. Crown 8vo, cloth, printed in Red and Black, 2s. 6d. net.

WILLIAM SHAKESPEARE: A Critical Study. By GEORGE BRANDES. In one volume, demy 8vo, 10s. net.

THE DRAMA: ADDRESSES By HENRY IRVING. With Portrait by J. McN. WHISTLER. Second Edition. Fcap. 8vo, 3s. 6d.

SOME INTERESTING FALLACIES OF THE MODERN STAGE. An Address delivered to the Playgoers' Club at St. James's Hall, on Sunday, 6th December 1891. By HERBERT BEERBOHM TREE. Crown 8vo, sewed, 6d. net.

LONDON : WILLIAM HEINEMANN
21 BEDFORD STREET, W.C.

WHEN WE DEAD AWAKEN

WHEN WE DEAD AWAKEN

A DRAMATIC EPILOGUE
In Three Acts

By HENRIK IBSEN

Translated by
WILLIAM ARCHER

LONDON: WILLIAM HEINEMANN

MCM

First Impression, March 1900
Second Impression, May 1900

CHARACTERS

Professor Arnold Rubek, *a sculptor.*

Mrs. Maia Rubek, *his wife.*

The Inspector at the Baths.

Ulfheim, *a landed proprietor.*

A Stranger Lady.

A Sister of Mercy.

Servants, Visitors to the Baths, Children, &c.

[*The First Act passes at a bathing establishment on the coast; the Second and Third Acts in the neighbourhood of a health resort high in the mountains.*]

WHEN WE DEAD AWAKEN

FIRST ACT

[*Outside the Bath Hotel. A portion of the main build-ing can be seen to the right. An open, park-like place with a fountain, groups of fine old trees, and shrubbery. To the left, a little pavilion almost covered with ivy and Virginia creeper. A table and chair outside it. At the back a view over the fjord, right out to sea, with headlands and small islands in the distance. It is a calm, warm and sunny summer morning.*]

[PROFESSOR RUBEK *and* MRS. MAIA RUBEK *are sitting in basket chairs beside a covered table on the lawn out-side the hotel, having just breakfasted. They have champagne and seltzer-water on the table, and each has a newspaper.* PROFESSOR RUBEK *is an elderly man of distinguished appearance, wearing a black*

A

velvet jacket, and for the rest in light summer attire. MAIA *is quite young, with a vivacious expression and lively, teasing eyes, yet with a suggestion of fatigue. She wears an elegant travelling dress.*]

MAIA.

[*sits for some time as though waiting for the* PROFESSOR *to say something, then lets her paper drop with a deep sigh*] Oh dear, dear, dear — !

PROFESSOR RUBEK.

[*looks up from his paper*] Well, Maia? What is the matter with you?

MAIA.

Just listen how silent it is here.

PROFESSOR RUBEK.

[*smiles indulgently*] And you can hear that?

MAIA.

What?

PROFESSOR RUBEK.

The silence?

MAIA.

Yes, indeed I can.

PROFESSOR RUBEK.

Well perhaps you are right, *mein Kind.* One can really hear the silence.

MAIA.

Heaven knows you can—when it's so absolutely overpowering as it is here—

PROFESSOR RUBEK.

Here at the Baths, you mean?

MAIA.

Everywhere at home here, it seems to me. Of course there was noise and bustle enough in the town. But I don't know how it is—even the noise and bustle seemed to have something dead about it.

PROFESSOR RUBEK.

[*with a searching glance*] You don't seem particularly glad to be at home again, Maia?

MAIA.

[*looks at him*] Are you glad?

PROFESSOR RUBEK.

[*evasively*] I—?

MAIA.

Yes, you, who have been so much, much further away than I. Are you entirely happy, now that you are at home again?

PROFESSOR RUBEK.

No—to be quite honest—perhaps not entirely happy.

MAIA.

[*with animation*] There, you see! Didn't I know it!

PROFESSOR RUBEK.

I have perhaps been too long abroad. I have drifted quite away from all this—this home life.

MAIA.

[*eagerly, drawing her chair nearer him*] There, you see, Rubek! We had much better get away again! As quickly as ever we can

PROFESSOR RUBEK.

[*somewhat impatiently*] Well, well, that is what we intend to do, my dear Maia. You know that.

MAIA.

But why not now—at once? Only think how

cosy and comfortable we could be down there, in our lovely new house—

PROFESSOR RUBEK.

[*with a forbearing smile*] We ought by rights to say: our lovely new h o m e—

MAIA.

[*shortly*] I prefer to say h o u s e—let us keep to that.

PROFESSOR RUBEK.

[*his eyes dwelling on her*] You are really a strange little creature.

MAIA.

Am I so strange?

PROFESSOR RUBEK.

Yes, I think so.

MAIA.

But why, pray? Perhaps because I'm not desperately in love with mooning about up here —?

PROFESSOR RUBEK.

Which of us was it that had absolutely set her heart upon our coming north this summer?

MAIA.

I admit, it was I.

PROFESSOR RUBEK.

It was certainly not I, at any rate.

MAIA.

But good heavens, who could have foreseen that everything would have altered so terribly at home here? And in such a short time, too! Why, it is only just four years since I went away—

PROFESSOR RUBEK.

Since you were married, yes.

MAIA.

Married? What has that to do with the matter?

PROFESSOR RUBEK.

[*continuing*]—since you became the Frau Professor, and found yourself mistress of a charming home—I beg your pardon—a very handsome house, I ought to say. And a villa on the Lake of Taunitz, just at the point that has become most fashionable, too—. In fact it is all very handsome and distinguished, Maia, there's no denying that. And spacious too. We need not always be treading on each other's heels.

MAIA.

[*lightly*] No, no, no—there's certainly no lack of house-room, and that sort of thing—

PROFESSOR RUBEK.

Remember, too, that you have been living in altogether more spacious and distinguished surroundings—in more polished society than you were accustomed to at home—

MAIA.

[*looking at him*] Ah, so you think it is *I* that have changed?

PROFESSOR RUBEK.

Indeed I do, Maia.

MAIA.

I alone? Not the people here?

PROFESSOR RUBEK.

Oh yes, they too—a little, perhaps. And not at all in the direction of amiability. That I readily admit.

MAIA.

I should think you must admit it, indeed.

PROFESSOR RUBEK.

[*changing the subject*] Do you know how it affects me when I look at the life of the people around us here?

MAIA.

No. Tell me.

PROFESSOR RUBEK.

It makes me think of that night we spent in the train, when we were coming up here—

MAIA.

Why, you were sound asleep all the time.

PROFESSOR RUBEK.

Not quite. I noticed how silent it became at all the little roadside stations. I heard the silence—like you, Maia—

MAIA.

Hm,—like me, yes.

PROFESSOR RUBEK.

—and that assured me that we had crossed the frontier—that we were really at home. For the train stopped at all the little stations—although there was nothing doing at all.

MAIA.

Then why did it stop—though there was nothing to be done?

PROFESSOR RUBEK.

Can't say. No one got out or in; but all the same the train stopped a long, endless time. And at every station I could make out that there were two railway men walking up and down the platform —one had a lantern in his hand—and they said things to each other in the night, low, and toneless, and meaningless.

MAIA.

Yes, that is quite true. There are always two men walking up and down, and talking—

PROFESSOR RUBEK.

—of nothing. [*Changing to a livelier tone*] But just wait till to-morrow. Then we shall have the great luxurious steamer coming up the harbour. We'll get on board her, and sail all round the coast —northward ho!—right to the polar sea.

MAIA.

Yes, but then you will see nothing of the country —and of the people. And that was what you particularly wanted.

PROFESSOR RUBEK.

[*short and snappishly*] I have seen more than enough.

MAIA.

Do you think a sea voyage will be better for you?

PROFESSOR RUBEK.

It is always a change.

MAIA.

Well well, if only it is the right thing for you—

PROFESSOR RUBEK.

For me? The right thing? There is nothing in the world the matter with me.

MAIA.

[*rises and goes up to him*] Yes, there is, Rubek. I am sure you must feel it yourself.

PROFESSOR RUBEK.

Why, my dearest Maia—what should be amiss with me?

MAIA.

[*behind him, bending over the back of his chair*] That you must tell me. You have begun to wander about without a moment's peace. You cannot rest anywhere—neither at home nor abroad. You have become quite misanthropic of late.

PROFESSOR RUBEK.

[*with a touch of sarcasm*] Dear me — have you noticed that?

MAIA.

No one that knows you can help noticing it. And then it seems to me so sad that you have lost all pleasure in your work.

PROFESSOR RUBEK.

That too, eh?

MAIA.

You that used to be so indefatigable—working morning to night!

PROFESSOR RUBEK.

[*gloomily*] Used to be, yes—

MAIA.

But ever since you got your great masterpiece out of hand—

PROFESSOR RUBEK.

[*nods thoughtfully*] "The Resurrection Day"—

MAIA.

—the masterpiece that has gone round the whole world, and made you so famous—

PROFESSOR RUBEK.

Perhaps that is just the misfortune, Maia.

MAIA.

How so?

PROFESSOR RUBEK.

When I had finished this masterpiece of mine— [*Makes a passionate movement with his hand*]—for "The Resurrection Day" is a masterpiece! Or was one in the beginning. No, it is one still. It must, must, must be a masterpiece.

MAIA.

[*looks at him in astonishment*] Why, Rubek—all the world knows that.

PROFESSOR RUBEK.

[*short, repellently*] All the world knows nothing! Understands nothing!

MAIA.

Well, at any rate it can divine something—

PROFESSOR RUBEK.

Something that isn't there at all, yes. Something
that never was in my mind. Ah yes, that they
can all go into ecstasies over.

[*Growling to himself*]

What is the good of working oneself to death for
the mob and the masses—for "all the world"!

MAIA.

Do you think it is better, then—do you think it is
worthy of you, to do nothing at all but a portrait
bust now and then?

PROFESSOR RUBEK.

[*with a sly smile*] They are not exactly portrait
busts that I turn out, Maia.

MAIA.

Yes, indeed they are—for the last two or three
years—ever since you finished your great group and
got it out of the house—

PROFESSOR RUBEK.

All the same, they are no mere portrait-busts, I
assure you.

MAIA.

What are they, then?

PROFESSOR RUBEK.

There is something equivocal, something cryptic, lurking in and behind these busts—a secret something, that the people themselves cannot see—

MAIA.

Indeed?

PROFESSOR RUBEK.

[*decisively*] I alone can see it. And it amuses me unspeakably.—On the surface I give them the "striking likeness," as they call it, that they all stand and gape at in astonishment—

[*Lowers his voice*]

—but at bottom they are all respectable, pompous horse-faces, and self-opinionated donkey-muzzles, and lop-eared, low-browed dog-skulls, and fatted swine-snouts—and sometimes dull, brutal bull-fronts as well.

MAIA.

[*indifferently*] All the dear domestic animals, in fact.

PROFESSOR RUBEK.

Simply the dear domestic animals, Maia. All the animals which men have bedevilled in their own image—and which have bedevilled men in return.

[*Empties his champagne-glass and laughs*]

And it is these double-faced works of art that our excellent plutocrats come and order of me. And pay for in all good faith—and in good round figures too —almost their weight in gold, as the saying goes.

MAIA.

[*fills his glass*] Come, Rubek! Drink and be happy.

PROFESSOR RUBEK.

[*passes his hand several times across his forehead and leans back in his chair*] I am happy, Maia. Really happy—in a way.

[*Short silence*]

For after all there is a certain happiness in feeling oneself free and independent on every hand—in having at one's command everything one can possibly wish for—all outward things, that is to say. Do you not agree with me, Maia?

MAIA.

Oh yes, I agree. All that is well enough in its way.

[*Looking at him*]

But do you remember what you promised me the day we came to an understanding on—on that difficult subject—

PROFESSOR RUBEK.

[*nods*]—the subject of our marriage, yes. It was rather a hard matter for you, Maia.

MAIA.

[*continuing unruffled*]—and agreed that I was to go abroad with you, and live there for good and all—and enjoy myself.—Do you remember what you promised me that day?

PROFESSOR RUBEK.

[*shaking his head*] No, I can't say that I do. Well, what did I promise?

MAIA.

You said you would take me up to a high mountain and show me all the glory of the world.

PROFESSOR RUBEK.

[*with a slight start*] Did I promise you that, too?

MAIA.

Me too? Who else, pray?

PROFESSOR RUBEK.

[*indifferently*] No, no, I only meant did I promise to show you—?

MAIA.

—all the glory of the world? Yes, you did. And all that glory should be mine, you said.

PROFESSOR RUBEK.

That is a sort of figure of speech that I was in the habit of using at one time.

MAIA.

Only a figure of speech?

PROFESSOR RUBEK.

Yes, a schoolboy phrase—the sort of thing I used to say when I wanted to lure the neighbours' children out to play with me, in the woods and on the mountains.

B

MAIA.

[*looking hard at him*] Perhaps you only wanted to lure me out to play, as well?

PROFESSOR RUBEK.

[*passing it off as a jest*] Well, has it not been a tolerably amusing game, Maia?

MAIA.

[*coldly*] I did not go with you only to play.

PROFESSOR RUBEK.

No, no, I daresay not.

MAIA.

And you never took me up with you to any high mountain, or showed me—

PROFESSOR RUBEK.

[*with irritation*]—all the glory of the world? No, I did not. For, let me tell you something: you are not really born to be a mountaineer, little Maia.

MAIA.

[*trying to control herself*] Yet at one time you seemed to think I was.

PROFESSOR RUBEK.

Four or five years ago, yes.

[*Stretching himself in his chair*]

Four or five years—it's a long, long time, Maia.

MAIA.

[*looking at him with a bitter expression*] Has the time seemed so very long to you, Rubek?

PROFESSOR RUBEK.

I am beginning now to find it a trifle long.

[*Yawning*]

Now and then, you know.

MAIA.

[*returning to her place*] I shall not bore you any longer.

> [*She resumes her seat, takes up the newspaper, and begins turning over the leaves. Silence on both sides.*]

PROFESSOR RUBEK.

[*leaning on his elbows across the table, and looking at her teasingly*] Is the Frau Professor offended?

Maia.

[*coldly, without looking up*] No, not at all.

> [*Visitors to the baths, most of them ladies, begin to pass, singly and in groups, through the park from the right, and out to the left.*]
> [WAITERS *bring refreshments from the hotel, and go off behind the pavilion.*]
> [*The* INSPECTOR, *wearing gloves and carrying a stick, comes from his rounds in the park, meets visitors, bows politely, and exchanges a few words with some of them.*]

The Inspector.

[*advancing to* PROFESSOR RUBEK's *table and politely taking off his hat*] I have the honour to wish you good morning, Mrs. Rubek.—Good morning, Professor Rubek.

Professor Rubek.

Good morning, good morning, Inspector.

The Inspector.

[*addressing himself to* MRS. RUBEK] May I venture to ask if you have slept well?

MAIA.

Yes, thank you; excellently—for my part. I always sleep like a stone.

THE INSPECTOR.

I am delighted to hear it. The first night in a strange place is often rather trying.—And the Professor—?

PROFESSOR RUBEK.

Oh, my night's rest is never much to boast of— especially of late.

THE INSPECTOR.

[*with a show of sympathy*] Oh—that is a pity. But after a few weeks' stay at the Baths—you will quite get over that.

PROFESSOR RUBEK.

[*looking up at him*] Tell me, Inspector—are any of your patients in the habit of taking baths during the night?

THE INSPECTOR.

[*astonished*] During the night? No, I have never heard of such a thing.

PROFESSOR RUBEK.

Have you not?

THE INSPECTOR.

No, I don't know of any one so ill as to require such treatment.

PROFESSOR RUBEK.

Well, at any rate there is some one who is in the habit of walking about the park by night?

THE INSPECTOR.

[*smiling and shaking his head*] No, Professor— that would be against the rules.

MAIA.

[*impatiently*] Good Heavens, Rubek I told you so this morning—you must have dreamt it!

PROFESSOR RUBEK.

[*drily*] Indeed? Must I? Thank you!

[*Turning to the* INSPECTOR]

The fact is, I got up last night—I couldn't| sleep —and I wanted to see what sort of night it was—

THE INSPECTOR.

[*attentively*] To be sure—and then—?

PROFESSOR RUBEK.

I looked out at the window—and caught sight of a white figure in there among the trees.

MAIA.

[*smiling to the* INSPECTOR] And the Professor declares that the figure was dressed in a bathing costume—

PROFESSOR RUBEK.

—or something like it, I said. I couldn't distinguish very clearly. But I am sure it was something white.

THE INSPECTOR.

Most remarkable. Was it a gentleman or a lady?

PROFESSOR RUBEK.

I could almost have sworn it was a lady. But then after it came another figure. And that one was quite dark—like a shadow—

THE INSPECTOR.

[*starting*] A dark one? Quite black, perhaps?

PROFESSOR RUBEK.

Yes, it certainly seemed so to me.

THE INSPECTOR.

[*a light breaking in upon him*] And behind the white figure? Following close upon her—?

PROFESSOR RUBEK.

Yes—at a little distance—

THE INSPECTOR.

Aha! Then I think I can explain the mystery, Professor.

PROFESSOR RUBEK.

Well, what was it then?

MAIA.

[*simultaneously*] Was the Professor really not dreaming?

THE INSPECTOR.

[*suddenly whispering, as he directs their attention towards the background on the right*] Hush, if you please! Look there.—Don't speak loud for a moment.

[*A slender lady, dressed in fine, cream-white cashmere, and followed by a Sister of Mercy in black, with a silver cross hanging by a chain on her breast, comes forward from behind the hotel and crosses the park towards the pavilion in front on the left. Her face is pale, and its lines seem to have stiffened, the eyelids are drooped and the eyes appear as though they saw nothing. Her dress comes down to her feet and clings to the body in perpendicular folds. Over her head, neck, breast, shoulders and arms she wears a large shawl of white crape. She keeps her arms crossed upon her breast. She carries her body immovably, and her steps are stiff and measured. The Sister's bearing is also measured, and she has the air of a servant. She keeps her brown piercing eyes incessantly fixed upon the lady.* WAITERS, *with napkins on their arms, come forward in the hotel doorway, and cast curious glances at the strangers, who take no notice of anything, and, without looking round, enter the pavilion.*]

PROFESSOR RUBEK.

[*has risen slowly and involuntarily, and stands staring at the closed door of the pavilion*] Who was that lady?

THE INSPECTOR.

She is a stranger who has rented the little pavilion there.

. PROFESSOR RUBEK.

A foreigner?

THE INSPECTOR.

Presumably.   At any rate they both came from abroad—about a week ago.   They have never been here before.

PROFESSOR RUBEK.

[*decidedly; looking at him*] It was she I saw in the park last night.

THE INSPECTOR.

No doubt it must have been.   I thought so from the first.

PROFESSOR RUBEK.

What is this lady's name, Inspector?

THE INSPECTOR.

She has registered herself as " Madame de Satow, with companion."   We know nothing more.

PROFESSOR RUBEK.

[*reflecting*] Satow? Satow—?

MAIA.

[*laughing mockingly*] Do you know any one of that name, Rubek? Eh?

PROFESSOR RUBEK.

[*shaking his head*] No, no one.—Satow? It sounds Russian—or at all events Slavonic. [*To the* INSPECTOR] What language does she speak?

THE INSPECTOR.

When the two ladies talk to each other, it is in a language I cannot make out at all. But at other times she speaks Norwegian like a native.

PROFESSOR RUBEK.

[*exclaims with a start*] Norwegian? You are sure you are not mistaken?

THE INSPECTOR.

No, how could I be mistaken in that?

PROFESSOR RUBEK.

[*looks at him with eager interest*] You have heard her yourself?

THE INSPECTOR.

Yes. I myself have spoken to her—several times.
—Only a few words, however; she is far from com-
municative. But—

PROFESSOR RUBEK.

But Norwegian it was?

THE INSPECTOR.

Thoroughly good Norwegian—perhaps with a little
north-country accent.

PROFESSOR RUBEK.

[*gazing straight before him in amazement, whispers*]
That too!

MAIA.

[*a little hurt and jarred*] Perhaps this lady has
been one of your models, Rubek? Search your
memory.

PROFESSOR RUBEK.

[*looks cuttingly at her*] Model!

MAIA.

[*with a provoking smile*] In your younger days, I
mean. You are said to have had such innumerable
models—long ago, of course.

PROFESSOR RUBEK.

[*in the same tone*] Oh no, little Frau Maia. I have in reality had only one single model. One and one only—for everything I have done.

THE INSPECTOR.

[*who has turned away and stands looking out to the left*] If you'll excuse me, I think I will take my leave. I see some one coming whom it is not particularly agreeable to meet. Especially in the presence of ladies.

PROFESSOR RUBEK.

[*looking in the same direction*] That sportsman there? Who is it?

THE INSPECTOR.

It is Squire Ulfheim, from—

PROFESSOR RUBEK.

Oh Squire Ulfheim—

THE INSPECTOR.

—the bear-killer, as they call him

PROFESSOR RUBEK

I know him.

THE INSPECTOR.

Who does not know him?

PROFESSOR RUBEK.

Very slightly, however.   Is he also among your patients—at last?

THE INSPECTOR.

No strangely enough—not as yet.   He comes here only once a year—on his way up to his hunting-grounds.—Excuse me for the moment—

[*Makes a movement to go into the hotel.*]

ULFHEIM'S VOICE.

[*heard outside*] Stop a moment, man!   Devil take it all, can't you stop?   Why do you always scuttle away from me?

THE INSPECTOR.

[*stops*] I am not scuttling at all, Mr. Ulfheim.

[ULFHEIM *enters from the left followed by a servant with a couple of sporting dogs in leash.   *ULFHEIM *is in shooting costume, with*

*high boots and a felt hat with a feather in it.
He is a long, lank, sinewy personage, with
matted hair and beard, and a loud voice.
His appearance gives no precise clue to his
age, but he is no longer young.*]

ULFHEIM.

[*pounces upon the* INSPECTOR] Is this a way to
receive strangers, hey? You scamper away with
your tail between your legs—as if you had the devil
at your heels.

THE INSPECTOR.

[*calmly, without answering him*] Has Mr. Ulfheim
arrived by the steamer?

ULFHEIM.

[*growls*] Haven't had the honour of seeing any
steamer. [*With his arms akimbo*] Do you mean to
say you don't know that *I* sail in my own cutter?

[*To the* SERVANT]

Look well after your fellow-creatures, Lars. But
take care you keep them ravenous, all the same.
Fresh meat-bones—but not too much meat on them,
do you hear? And be sure it's reeking raw, and

bloody.   And get something in your own belly while you're about it.

[*Aiming a kick at him*]

Now then, go to hell with you !

[*The* SERVANT *goes out with the dogs, behind the corner of the hotel.*]

THE INSPECTOR.

Would not Mr. Ulfheim like to go into the dining-room in the meantime ?

ULFHEIM.

In among all the half-dead flies and people ?   No, thank you a thousand times, Mr. Inspector.

THE INSPECTOR.

Well, well, please yourself.

ULFHEIM.

But get the housekeeper to prepare a hamper for me as usual.   There must be plenty of provender in it—and lots of brandy—!   You can tell her that I or Lars will come and play Old Harry with her if she doesn't—

THE INSPECTOR.

[*interrupting*] We know your ways of old.

[*Turning*] Can I give the waiter any orders, Professor? Can I send Mrs. Rubek anything?

PROFESSOR RUBEK.

No thank you; nothing for me.

MAIA.

Nor for me.

[*The* INSPECTOR *goes into the hotel.*]

ULFHEIM.

[*stares at them a moment; then lifts his hat*] Why, blast me if here isn't a country tyke that has strayed into regular tip-top society.

PROFESSOR RUBEK.

[*looking up*] What do you mean by that, Mr. Ulfheim?

ULFHEIM.

[*more quietly and politely*] I believe I have the honour of addressing no less a person than the great Sculptor Rubek.

PROFESSOR RUBEK.

[*nods*] I remember meeting you once or twice— the autumn when I was last at home.

C

ULFHEIM.

That's many years ago now, though. And then
you weren't so illustrious as I hear you've since
become. At that time even a dirty bear-hunter
might venture to come near you.

PROFESSOR RUBEK.

[*smiling*] I don't bite even now.

MAIA.

[*looks with interest at* ULFHEIM] Are you really
and truly a bear-hunter?

ULFHEIM.

[*seating himself at the next table, nearer the hotel*]
A bear-hunter when I · have the chance, madam.
But I make the best of any sort of game that comes
in my way—eagles, and wolves, and women, and
elks, and reindeer—if only it's fresh and juicy and
has plenty of blood in it—[*Drinks ʾfrom his pocket-
flask*]

MAIA.

[*regarding him fixedly*] But you like bear-hunting
best?

ULFHEIM.

I like it best, yes. For then one can have the
knife handy at a pinch. [*With a slight smile*] We

both work in a hard material, madam—both your husband and I. He struggles with his marble blocks, I daresay; and I struggle with tense and quivering bear-sinews. And we both of us win the fight in the end — subdue and master our material. We don't give in until we have got the better of it, though it fight never so hard.

PROFESSOR RUBEK.

[*deep in thought*] There's a great] deal of truth in what you say.

ULFHEIM.

Yes, for the stone has something to fight for too, I take it. It is dead, and determined with all its might not to let itself be hammered into life. Just like the bear when you come and prod *it* up in its lair.

MAIA.

Are you going up into the forests now to hunt?

ULFHEIM.

I am going right up into the high mountains.—I suppose you have never been in the high mountains, madam?

MAIA.

No, never.

ULFHEIM.

Confound it all then, you must be sure and come up there this very summer! I'll take you with me —both you and the Professor, with pleasure.

MAIA.

Thanks. But Rubek is thinking of taking a sea trip this summer.

PROFESSOR RUBEK.

Round the coast—through the island channels.

·ULFHEIM.

Ugh — what the devil would you do in those damnable sickly gutters—floundering about in the brackish ditchwater? Dishwater I should rather call it.

MAIA.

There, you hear, Rubek!

ULFHEIM.

No, much better come up with me to the mountains—away, clean away, from the trail and taint of men. You can't think what that means for me. But such a little lady—[*He stops*]

    [*The Sister of Mercy comes out of the pavilion and goes into the hotel.*]

ULFHEIM.

[*following her with his eyes*] Just look at her, do! That night-crow there!—Who is it that's to be buried?

PROFESSOR RUBEK.

I have not heard of any one—

ULFHEIM.

Well, there's some one on the point of giving up the ghost, then—in one corner or another.—People that are sickly and rickety should have the goodness to see about getting themselves buried—the sooner the better.

MAIA.

Have you ever been ill yourself, Mr. Ulfheim?

ULFHEIM.

Never. If I had, I shouldn't be here.—But my nearest friends—they have been ill, poor things.

MAIA.

And what did you do for your nearest friends?

ULFHEIM.

Shot them of course.

PROFESSOR RUBEK.

[*looking at him*] Shot them ?

MAIA.

[*moving her chair back*] Shot them dead?

ULFHEIM.

[*nods*] I never miss, madam.

MAIA.

But how can you possibly shoot people !

ULFHEIM.

I am not speaking of people—

MAIA.

You said your nearest friends—

ULFHEIM.

Well, who should that be but my dogs?

MAIA.

Are your dogs your nearest friends?

ULFHEIM.

I have none nearer. My honest, trusty, absolutely
loyal comrades—. When one of them turns sick

and miserable—bang!—and there's my friend sent packing—to the other world.

> [*The Sister of Mercy comes out of the hotel with a tray on which is bread and milk. She places it on the table outside the pavilion, which she enters.*]

ULFHEIM.

[*laughs scornfully*] That stuff there—is that what you call food for human beings! Milk and water and soft, clammy bread. Ah, you should see my comrades feeding! Should you like to see it?

MAIA.

[*smiling across to the* PROFESSOR *and rising*] Yes, very much.

ULFHEIM.

[*also rising*] Spoken like a woman of spirit, madam! Come with me, then! They swallow whole great thumping meat-bones—gulp them up and then gulp them down again. Oh, it's a regular treat to see them. Come along. and I'll show you—and while we're about it, we can talk over this trip to the mountains—

> [*He goes out by the corner of the hotel,* MAIA *following him.*]

[*Almost at the same moment the Strange Lady comes out of the pavilion and seats herself at the table.*]

[*The Lady raises her glass of milk and is about to drink, but stops and looks across at* RUBEK *with vacant, expressionless eyes.*]

PROFESSOR RUBEK.

[*remains sitting at his table and gazes fixedly and earnestly at her. At last he rises, goes some steps towards her, stops, and says in a low voice*] I know you quite well, Irene.

THE LADY.

[*in a toneless voice, setting down her glass*] You can guess who I am, Arnold?

PROFESSOR RUBEK.

[*without answering*] And you recognise me too, I see.

THE LADY.

With you it is quite another matter.

PROFESSOR RUBEK.

With me?—How so?

THE LADY.

Oh, you are still alive.

PROFESSOR RUBEK.

[*not understanding*] Alive—?

THE LADY.

[*after a short pause*] Who was the other? The woman you had with you—there at the table?

PROFESSOR RUBEK.

[*a little reluctantly*] She? That was my — my wife.

THE LADY.

[*nods slowly*] Indeed. That is well, Arnold. Some one, then, who does not concern me—

PROFESSOR RUBEK.

[*nods*] No, of course not—

THE LADY.

—one whom you have taken to you after my lifetime.

PROFESSOR RUBEK.

[*suddenly looking hard at her*] After your—? What do you mean by that, Irene?

IRENE.

[*without answering*] And the child? The child is prospering too. Our child survives me—and has come to honour and glory.

PROFESSOR RUBEK.

[*smiles as at a far-off recollection*] Our child? Yes, we called it so—then.

IRENE.

In my lifetime.

PROFESSOR RUBEK.

[*trying to take a lighter tone*] Yes, Irene — I can assure you " our child " has become famous all the wide world over. I suppose you have read about it.

IRENE.

[*nods*] And has made its father famous too.—That was your dream.

PROFESSOR RUBEK.

[*more softly, with emotion*] It *is* to you I owe everything, everything, Irene—and I thank you.

IRENE.

[*lost in thought for a moment*] If I had then done what I had a right to do, Arnold—

PROFESSOR RUBEK.

Well? What then?

IRENE.

I should have killed that child.

PROFESSOR RUBEK.

Killed it, you say?

IRENE.

[*whispering*] Killed it—before I went away from you. Crushed it—crushed *it* to dust.

PROFESSOR RUBEK.

[*shakes his head reproachfully*] You would never have been able to, Irene. You had not the heart to do it.

IRENE.

No, in those days I had not that sort of heart.

PROFESSOR RUBEK.

But since then? Afterwards?

IRENE.

Since then I have killed it innumerable times. By daylight and in the dark. Killed it in hatred— and in revenge—and in anguish.

Professor Rubek.

[*goes close up to the table and asks softly*] Irene—tell me now at last—after all these years—why did you go away from me? You disappeared so utterly—left not a trace behind

Irene.

[*shaking her head slowly*] Oh Arnold—why should I tell you that now—from the world beyond the grave?

Professor Rubek.

Was there some one else whom you had come to love?

Irene.

There was one who had no longer any use for my love—any use for my life.

Professor Rubek.

[*changing the subject*] Hm—don't let us talk any more of the past.

Irene.

No, no—by all means don't let us talk of what is beyond the grave—what is now beyond the grave for me.

PROFESSOR RUBEK.

Where have you been, Irene? All my inquiries were fruitless—you seemed to have vanished away.

IRENE.

I went into the darkness—when the child stood transfigured in the light.

PROFESSOR RUBEK.

Have you travelled much about the world?

IRENE.

Yes. Travelled in many lands.

PROFESSOR RUBEK.

[*looks compassionately at her*] And what have you found to do, Irene?

IRENE.

[*turning her eyes upon him*] Wait a little; let me see—. Yes, now I have it. I have posed on the turntable in variety-shows. Posed as a naked statue in living pictures. Raked in heaps of money. That was more than I could do with you; for you had none.—And then I have turned the heads of all sorts of men. That, too, was more than I could do with you, Arnold. You kept yourself better in hand.

PROFESSOR RUBEK.

[*hastening to pass the subject by*] And then you have married, too?

IRENE.

Yes; I married one of them.

PROFESSOR RUBEK.

Who is your husband?

IRENE.

He was a South American. A distinguished diplomatist. [*Looks straight in front of her with a stony smile*] Him I managed to drive quite out of his mind; mad—incurably mad; inexorably mad.— It was great sport, I can tell you—while it was in the doing. I could have laughed within me all the time—if I had anything within me.

PROFESSOR RUBEK.

And where is he now?

IRENE.

Oh, in a churchyard somewhere or other. With a fine handsome monument over him. And with a bullet rattling in his skull.

PROFESSOR RUBEK.

Did he kill himself?

IRENE.

Yes, he was good enough to take that off my hands.

PROFESSOR RUBEK.

Do you not lament his loss, Irene?

IRENE.

[*not understanding*] Lament? What loss?

PROFESSOR RUBEK.

Why, the loss of Herr von Satow, of course.

IRENE.

His name was not Satow.

PROFESSOR RUBEK.

Was it not?

IRENE.

My second husband is called Satow. He is a Russian—

PROFESSOR RUBEK.

And where is he?

IRENE.

Far away in the Ural Mountains. Among all his gold-mines.

PROFESSOR RUBEK.

So he lives there?

IRENE.

[*shrugs her shoulders*] Lives? Lives? In reality I have killed him—

PROFESSOR RUBEK.

[*starts*] Killed—!

IRENE.

Killed him with a fine sharp dagger which I always have with me in bed—

PROFESSOR RUBEK.

[*vehemently*] I don't believe you, Irene.

IRENE.

[*with a gentle smile*] Indeed you may believe it, Arnold.

PROFESSOR RUBEK.

[*looks compassionately at her*] Have you never had a child?

IRENE.

Yes, I have had many children.

PROFESSOR RUBEK

And where are your children now?

IRENE.

I killed them.

PROFESSOR RUBEK.

[*severely*] Now you are telling me lies again.

IRENE.

I have killed them, I tell you—murdered them pitilessly. As soon as ever they came into the world. Oh, long, long before. One after the other.

PROFESSOR RUBEK.

[*sadly and earnestly*] There is something hidden behind everything you say.

IRENE.

How can I help that? Every word I say is whispered into my ear.

D

PROFESSOR RUBEK.

I believe I am the only one that can divine your meaning.

IRENE.

Surely you ought to be the only one.

PROFESSOR RUBEK.

[*rests his hands on the table and looks intensely at her*] Some of the strings of your nature have broken.

IRENE.

[*gently*] Does not that always happen when a young warm-blooded woman dies?

PROFESSOR RUBEK.

Oh Irene, shake off these wild imaginings—! You are living! Living—living !

IRENE.

[*rises slowly from her chair and says, quivering*] I was dead for many years. They came and bound me—laced my arms together at my back.—Then they lowered me into a grave-vault, with iron bars before the loop-hole. And with padded walls—so that no one on the earth above could hear the grave-shrieks. But now I am beginning, in a way, to rise from the dead.

[*She seats herself again*]

PROFESSOR RUBEK.

[*after a pause*] In all this, do you hold me guilty?

IRENE.

Yes.

PROFESSOR RUBEK.

Guilty of that—your death, as you call it.

IRENE.

Guilty of the fact that I had to die.

[*Changing her tone to one of indifference*]

Why don't you sit down, Arnold?

PROFESSOR RUBEK.

May I?

IRENE.

Yes.—Do not be afraid of being frozen. I don't think I am quite turned to ice yet.

PROFESSOR RUBEK.

[*moves a chair and seats himself at her table*] There, Irene. Now we two are sitting together as in the old days.

IRENE.

At a little distance from each other—also as in the old days.

PROFESSOR RUBEK.

[*moving nearer*] It had to be so, then.

IRENE.

Had it?

PROFESSOR RUBEK.

[*decisively*] There had to be a distance between us—

IRENE.

Was it absolutely necessary, Arnold?

PROFESSOR RUBEK.

[*continuing*] Do you remember what you answered when I asked if you would go with me out into the wide world?

IRENE.

I held up three fingers in the air and swore that I
would go with you to the world's end and to the end
of life. And that I would serve you in all things—

PROFESSOR RUBEK.

As the model for my art—

IRENE.

—in frank, utter nakedness—

PROFESSOR RUBEK.

[*with emotion*] And you did serve me, Irene—so
joyously—so gladly and ungrudgingly.

IRENE.

Yes, with all the pulsing blood of my youth, I
served you!

PROFESSOR RUBEK.

[*nodding, with a look of gratitude*] That you have
every right to say.

IRENE.

I fell down at your feet and served you, Arnold!

[*Holding her clenched hand towards him*]

But you, you, you—!

PROFESSOR RUBEK.

[*defensively*] I never did you any wrong ! Never, Irene !

IRENE.

Yes, you did ! You did wrong to my innermost, inborn nature—

PROFESSOR RUBEK.

[*starting back*] I—!

IRENE.

Yes, you ! I exposed myself wholly and unreservedly to your gaze—

[*More softly*]

And never once did you touch me.

PROFESSOR RUBEK.

Irene, did you not understand that many a time I was almost beside myself under the spell of all your loveliness ?

IRENE.

[*continuing undisturbed*] And yet—if you had touched me, I think I should have killed you on the

spot. For I had a sharp needle always upon me—
hidden in my hair—

[*Strokes her forehead meditatively*]

But after all—after all—that you could—

PROFESSOR RUBEK.

[*looks impressively at her*] I was an artist, Irene.

IRENE.

[*darkly*] That is just it. That is just it.

PROFESSOR RUBEK.

An artist first of all. And I was sick with the
desire to achieve the great work of my life. [*Losing
himself in recollection*] It was to be called "The
Resurrection Day"—figured in the likeness of a
young woman, awakening from the sleep of death—

IRENE.

Our child, yes—

PROFESSOR RUBEK.

[*continuing*] It was to be the awakening of the
noblest, purest, most ideal woman the world ever
saw. Then I found you. You were what I required
in every respect. And you consented so willingly—

so gladly. You renounced home and kindred—and went with me.

IRENE.

To go with you meant for me the resurrection of my childhood.

PROFESSOR RUBEK.

That was just why I found in you all that I required—in you as in no one else. I came to look on you as a thing hallowed. You became for me a sacred being, not to be touched save in adoring thoughts. In those days I was still young, Irene. And the superstition took hold of me that if I touched you, if I desired you with my senses, my soul would be profaned, so that I should be unable to accomplish what I was striving for.—And I still think there was some truth in that.

IRENE.

[*nods with a touch of scorn*] The work of art first —after it the human being.

PROFESSOR RUBEK.

You must judge me as you will; but at that time I was utterly dominated by my great task—and exultantly happy in it.

IRENE.

And you achieved your great task, Arnold.

PROFESSOR RUBEK.

Thanks and praise be to you, I achieved my great task. I wanted to embody the pure woman as I saw her awakening on the Resurrection Day. Not marvelling at anything new and unknown and un-divined; but filled with a sacred joy at finding herself unchanged—she, the woman of earth—in the higher, freer, happier region—after the long, dreamless sleep of death.

[*More softly*]

Thus did I fashion her.—I fashioned her in your image, Irene.

IRENE.

[*laying her hands flat upon the table and leaning against the back of her chair*] And then you were done with me—

PROFESSOR RUBEK.

[*reproachfully*] Irene!

IRENE.

You had no longer any use for me—

PROFESSOR RUBEK.

How can you say that!

IRENE.

—and began to look about you for other ideals.

PROFESSOR RUBEK.

I found none, none after you.

IRENE.

And no other models, Arnold?

PROFESSOR RUBEK.

You were no model to me. You were the fountain head of my achievement.

IRENE.

[*is silent for a short time*] What poems have you made since? In marble I mean. Since the day I left you.

PROFESSOR RUBEK.

I have made no poems since that day — only frittered away my life in modelling.

IRENE.

And that woman, whom you are now living with—?

PROFESSOR RUBEK.

[*interrupting vehemently*] Do not speak of her now! It makes me tingle with shame.

IRENE.

Where are you thinking of going with her?

PROFESSOR RUBEK.

[*slack and weary*] Oh, on a tedious coasting voyage to the North, I suppose.

IRENE.

[*looks at him, smiles almost imperceptibly, and whispers*] You should rather go high up into the mountains. As high as ever you can. Higher higher,—always higher, Arnold.

PROFESSOR RUBEK.

[*with eager expectation*] Are you going up there?

IRENE.

Have you the courage to meet me once again?

Professor Rubek.

[*struggling with himself, uncertainly*] If we could—
oh, if only we could—ⁱ

Irene.

Why can we not do what we will?
[*Looks at him and whispers beseechingly with
ᵖfolded hands*]
Come, come, Arnold! Oh, come up to me—ⁱ

[Maia *enters, glowing with pleasure, from behind
the hotel, and goes quickly up to the table
where they were previously sitting*]

Maia.

[*still at the corner of the hotel, without looking
around*] Oh, you may say what you please, Rubek,
but—[*Stops, as she catches sight of* Irene]—Oh,
I beg your pardon—I see you have made an
acquaintance.

Professor Rubek.

[*curtly*] Renewed an acquaintance. [*Rises*] What
was it you wanted with me?

MAIA.

I only wanted to say this : you may do whatever you please, but *I* am not going with you on that disgusting steamboat.

PROFESSOR RUBEK.

Why not ?

MAIA.

Because I want to go up on the mountains and into the forests—that's what I want. [*Insinuatingly*] Oh, you must let me do it, Rubek.—I shall be so good, so good afterwards.

PROFESSOR RUBEK.

Who is it that has put these ideas *in*to your head ?

MAIA.

Why he—that horrid bear-k*i*ller.—Oh, you cannot conceive all the marvellous things he has to tell about the mountains. And about l*i*fe up there! They're ugly, horrid, repulsive, most of the yarns he sp*i*ns—for I almost believe he's lying—but wonderfully alluring all the same. Oh, won't you let me go with him ? Only to see if it's true what he says, you understand. May I, Rubek ?

PROFESSOR RUBEK.

Yes, I have not the slightest objection. Off you go to the mountains—as far and as long as you please. I shall perhaps be going the same way myself.

MAIA.

[*quickly*] No, no, no, you needn't do that! Not on my account!

PROFESSOR RUBEK.

I want to go to the mountains. I have made up my mind to go.

MAIA.

Oh thanks, thanks! May I tell the bear-killer at once.

PROFESSOR RUBEK.

Tell the bear-killer whatever you please.

MAIA.

Oh thanks, thanks, thanks! *Is about to take his*

hand; he repels the movement] Oh, how dear and good you are to-day, Rubek!

[*She runs into the hotel.*]

[*At the same time the door of the pavilion is softly and noiselessly set ajar. The Sister of Mercy stands in the opening, intently on the watch. No one sees her.*]

PROFESSOR RUBEK.

[*decidedly, turning to* IRENE] Shall we meet up there then?

IRENE.

[*rising slowly*] Yes, we shall certainly meet.—I have sought for you so long.

PROFESSOR RUBEK.

When did you begin to seek for me, Irene?

IRENE.

[*with a touch of jesting bitterness*] From the time when I realised that I had given away to you something rather indispensable, Arnold. Something one ought never to part with.

PROFESSOR RUBEK.

[*bowing his head*] Yes, that is bitterly true. You gave me three or four years of your youth.

IRENE.

More, more than that I gave you—spendthrift as I then was.

PROFESSOR RUBEK.

Yes, you were prodigal, Irene. You gave me all your naked loveliness—

IRENE.

—to gaze upon—

PROFESSOR RUBEK.

—and to glorify—

IRENE.

Yes, for your own glorification.—And the child's.

PROFESSOR RUBEK.

And yours too, Irene.

IRENE.

But you have forgotten the most precious gift.

PROFESSOR RUBEK.

The most precious—? What gift was that?

IRENE.

I gave you my young, living soul. And that gift
left me empty within—soulless.

[*Looking at him with a fixed stare*]

It was that I died of, Arnold.
[*The Sister of Mercy opens the door wide and
makes room for her. She goes into the
pavilion.*]

PROFESSOR RUBEK.

[*stands and looks after her; then whispers*] Irene!

E

SECOND ACT

[*Near a mountain health resort. The landscape stretches in the form of an immense treeless upland towards a long mountain lake. Beyond the lake rises a range of peaks with blue-white snow in the clefts. In the foreground on the left a purling brook falls in severed streamlets down a steep wall of rock, and thence flows smoothly over the upland until it disappears to the right. Dwarf trees, plants, and stones along the course of the brook. In the foreground on the right a hillock, with a stone bench on the top of it. It is a summer afternoon, towards sunset.*]

[*At some distance over the upland, on the other side of the brook, a troop of children is singing, dancing, and playing. Some are dressed in peasant costume, others in town-made clothes. Their happy laughter is heard, softened by distance, during the following.*]

66

[PROFESSOR RUBEK *is sitting on the bench, with a plaid over his shoulders, and looking down at the children's play.*]

[*Presently* MAIA *comes forward from among some bushes on the upland to the left, well back, and . scans the prospect with her hand shading her eyes. She wears a flat tourist cap, a short skirt, kilted up, reaching only midway between ankle and knee, and high, stout lace-boots. She has in her hand a long alpenstock.*]

MAIA.

[*at last catches sight of* RUBEK *and calls*] Hallo!

[*She advances over the upland, jumps over the brook, with the aid of her alpenstock, and climbs up the hillock.*]

MAIA.

[*panting*] Oh, how I have been rushing around looking for you, Rubek.

PROFESSOR RUBEK.

[*nods indifferently and asks*] Have you just come from the hotel?

MAIA.

Yes, that was the last place I tried—that fly-trap.

PROFESSOR RUBEK.

[*looking at her for a moment*] I noticed that you were not at the dinner-table.

MAIA.

No, we had our dinner in the open air, we two.

PROFESSOR RUBEK.

" We two " ?   What two?

MAIA.

Why, I and that horrid bear-killer, of course.

PROFESSOR RUBEK.

Oh, he.

MAIA.

Yes.   And first thing to-morrow morning we are going off again.

PROFESSOR RUBEK.

After bears ?

MAIA.

Yes.   Off to kill bruin.

PROFESSOR RUBEK.

Have you found the tracks of any ?

MAIA.

[*with superiority*] You don't suppose that bears are to be found in the naked mountains, do you?

PROFESSOR RUBEK.

Where then?

MAIA.

Far beneath. On the lower slopes; in the thickest parts of the forest. Places that are quite impenetrable for ordinary town-folk—

PROFESSOR RUBEK.

And you two are going down there to-morrow?

MAIA.

[*throwing herself down among the heather*] Yes, so we have arranged.—Or perhaps we may start this evening.—If you have no objection, that's to say?

PROFESSOR RUBEK.

I? Far be it from me to—

MAIA.

[*quickly*] Of course Lars goes with us—with the dogs.

PROFESSOR RUBEK.

I have not solicited any information on the subject of Mr. Lars and his dogs.

[*Changing the subject*]

Should you not prefer to sit properly on the seat?

MAIA.

[*drowsily*] No, thank you. I'm lying so delightfully in the soft heather.

PROFESSOR RUBEK.

I can see that you are tired.

MAIA.

[*yawning*] I almost think I'm beginning to feel tired.

PROFESSOR RUBEK.

That always comes afterwards—when the excitement is over—

MAIA.

[*in a drowsy tone*] Yes, I will lie and close my eyes.

[*A short pause*]

MAIA.

[*with sudden impatience*] Ugh, Rubek—how can you bear to sit and listen to those children's screams! And to watch all the capers they are cutting, too!

PROFESSOR RUBEK.

There is something harmonious—almost like music —in their movements, now and then ; amid all the clumsiness. And it amuses me to sit and watch for these isolated moments—when they come.

MAIA.

[*with a somewhat scornful laugh*] Yes, you are always, always an artist.

PROFESSOR RUBEK.

And I propose to remain one.

MAIA.

[*lying on her side, so that her back is turned to him*] There's not a bit of the artist about him.

PROFESSOR RUBEK.

[*with attention*] Who is *it* that's not an artist ?

MAIA.

[*again in a sleepy tone*] Why he—the other one, of course.

PROFESSOR RUBEK.

The bear-hunter, you mean ?

MAIA.

Yes. There's not a bit of the artist about him—
not the least little bit.

PROFESSOR RUBEK.

[*smiling*] No, I believe there's no doubt about
that.

MAIA.

[*vehemently, without moving*] And so ugly as he is!

[*Plucks up a tuft of heather and throws it away*]

So ugly, so ugly! Isch!

PROFESSOR RUBEK.

Is that why you are so ready to set off with him—
out into the wilds?

MAIA.

[*curtly*] I don't know.

[*Turning towards him*]

You are ugly too, Rubek.

PROFESSOR RUBEK.

Have you only just discovered it?

MAIA.

No, I have seen it for long.

Professor Rubek.

[*shrugging his shoulders*] One grows old. One grows old, Frau Maia.

Maia.

It's not that sort of ugliness that I mean at all. But there has come to be such an expression of fatigue, of utter weariness, in your eyes—when you deign, once in a while, to cast a glance at me.

Professor Rubek.

Have you noticed that?

Maia.

[*nods*] Little by little this evil look has come into your eyes. It seems almost as though you were nursing some dark plot against me.

Professor Rubek.

Indeed?

[*In a friendly but earnest tone*]

Come here and sit beside me, Maia; and let us talk a little.

Maia.

[*half rising*] Then will you let me sit upon your knee? As I used to in the early days?

·Professor Rubek.

No, you mustn't—people can see us from the hotel.

[*Moves a little*]

But you can sit here on the bench—at my side.

Maia.

No, thank you ; in that case I'd rather lie here, where I am.   I can hear you quite well here.

[*Looks inquiringly at him*]

Well, what *is* it you want to say to me ?

Professor Rubek.

[*begins slowly*] What do you think was my real reason for agreeing to make this tour ?

Maia.

Well—I remember you declared among other things, that it was going to do m e such a tremendous lot of good.   But—but—

Professor Rubek.

But—?

Maia.

But now I˙don't believe the least little bit that that was the reason—

·PROFESSOR RUBEK.

Then what is your theory about it now?

MAIA.

I think now that it was on account of that pale lady.

PROFESSOR RUBEK.

Madame von Satow—!

MAIA.

Yes, she who is always hanging at our heels. Yesterday evening she made her appearance up here too.

PROFESSOR RUBEK.

But what in all the world—!

MAIA.

Oh, I know you knew her very well indeed—long before you knew me.

PROFESSOR RUBEK.

And had forgotten her, too—long before I knew you.

MAIA.

[*sitting upright*] Can you forget so easily, Rubek?

PROFESSOR RUBEK.

[*curtly*] Yes, very easily indeed.

[*Adds harshly*]

When I want to forget.

MAIA.

Even a woman who has been a model to you?

PROFESSOR RUBEK.

When I have no longer any use for her——

MAIA.

One who has stood to you unclothed?

PROFESSOR RUBEK.

That means nothing—nothing for us artists.

[*With a change of tone*]

And then—may I venture to ask—how was *I* to guess that she was in this country?

MAIA.

Oh, you might have seen her name in a Visitors' List—in one of the newspapers.

PROFESSOR RUBEK.

But I had no idea of the name she now goes by. I had never heard of any Herr von Satow.

MAIA.

[*affecting weariness*] Oh well then, I suppose it must have been for some other reason that you were so set upon this journey.

PROFESSOR RUBEK.

[*seriously*] Yes, Maia—it was for another reason. A quite different reason. And that is what we must sooner or later have a clear explanation about.

MAIA.

[*in a fit of suppressed laughter*] Heavens, how solemn you look!

PROFESSOR RUBEK.

[*suspiciously scrutinising her*] Yes, perhaps a little more solemn than necessary.

MAIA.

How so—?

PROFESSOR RUBEK.

And that is a very good thing for us both.

MAIA.

You begin to make me feel curious, Rubek.

PROFESSOR RUBEK.

Only curious?   Not a little bit uneasy.

MAIA.

[*shaking her head*] Not in the least.

PROFESSOR RUBEK.

Good.   Then listen.—You said that day down at
the Baths that it seemed to you I had become very
nervous of late—

MAIA.

Yes, and you really have.

·PROFESSOR RUBEK.

And what do you think can be the reason of that?

MAIA.

How can I tell—?

[*Quickly*]

Perhaps you have grown tired of this constant
companionship with me.

PROFESSOR RUBEK.

Constant—?   Why not say " everlasting " ?

MAIA.

Daily companionship, then. Here have we two solitary people lived down there for four or five mortal years, and scarcely been an hour away. from each other.—We two all by ourselves.

PROFESSOR RUBEK.

[*with interest*] Well? And then—?

MAIA.

[*a little oppressed*] You are not a particularly sociable man, Rubek. Your tendency is to keep yourself to yourself and think your own thoughts. And of course I can't talk properly to you about your affairs. I know nothing about art and that sort of thing—

[*With an impatient gesture*]

And care very little either, for that matter.

PROFESSOR RUBEK.

Well, well; and that's why we sit for the most part by the fireside, and chat of your affairs.

MAIA.

Oh, good gracious—I have no affairs to chat about.

PROFESSOR RUBEK.

Well, they are trifles, perhaps ; but at any rate the time passes for us in that way as well as another, Maia.

MAIA.

Yes, you are right. Time passes. It is passing away from you, Rubek.—And I suppose it is really that that makes you so uneasy.

PROFESSOR RUBEK.

[*nods vehemently*] And so restless !

[*Writhing in his seat*]

No, I shall soon not be able to endure this pitiful life any longer.

MAIA.

[*rises and stands for a moment looking at him*] If you want to get rid of me, you have only to say so.

·PROFESSOR RUBEK.

Why will you use such phrases ? Get rid of you ?

MAIA.

Yes, if you want to have done with me, please say so right out. And I will go that instant.

PROFESSOR RUBEK.

[*with an almost imperceptible smile*] Do you intend that as a threat, Maia?

MAIA.

There can be no threat for you in what I said.

PROFESSOR RUBEK.

[*rising*] No, I confess you are right there.

[*Adds after a pause*]

You and I cannot possibly go on living together like this—

MAIA.

Well? And then—?

PROFESSOR RUBEK.

There is no " then " about it.

[*With emphasis on his words*]

Because we two cannot go on living together alone —it does not necessarily follow that we must part.

MAIA.

[*smiles scornfully*] Only draw away from each other a little, you mean?

F

PROFESSOR RUBEK.

[*shakes his head*] Even that is not necessary.

MAIA.

Well then? Come out with what you want to do with me.

PROFESSOR RUBEK.

[*with some hesitation*] What I now feel so keenly —and so painfully—that I require, is to have some one about me who stands really and absolutely close to me—

MAIA.

[*interrupts him anxiously*] Don't *I* do that, Rubek?

PROFESSOR RUBEK.

[*waving her aside*] Not in that sense. What I need *is* the companionship of another person who can, as it were, complete me—supply what is wanting in me—be one with me in all my striving.

MAIA.

[*slowly*] It's true that in hard things like that I can't be of any use to you.

PROFESSOR RUBEK.

Oh no, that's not at all in your line, Maia.

MAIA.

[*with an outburst*] And heaven knows I don't want it to be, either.

PROFESSOR RUBEK.

I know that very well.—And it was with no idea of finding any such help in my life-work that I married you.

MAIA.

[*observing him closely*] I can see in your face that you are thinking of some one else.

PROFESSOR RUBEK.

Indeed? I have never noticed before that you were a thought-reader. But you can see that, can you?

MAIA.

Yes, I can. Oh, I know you so well, so well, Rubek.

PROFESSOR RUBEK.

Then perhaps you can also see who it is I am thinking of?

MAIA.

Yes, indeed I can.

PROFESSOR RUBEK.

Well?   Have the goodness to—?

MAIA.

You are thinking of that—that model you once used for—

[*Suddenly letting slip the train of thought*]

Do you know, the people down at the hotel think she's mad.

PROFESSOR RUBEK.

Indeed?   And pray what do the people down at the hotel think of you and the bear-killer?

MAIA.

That has nothing to do with the matter.

[*Continuing the former train of thought*]

But it was this pale lady you were thinking of.

PROFESSOR RUBEK.

[*calmly*] Precisely, of her.—When I no longer had any use for her—and when, besides, she went away from me—vanished without a word—

MAIA.

Then you accepted me as a sort of makeshift, I suppose?

PROFESSOR RUBEK.

[*more unfeelingly*] Something of the sort, to tell the truth, little Maia. For a year or a year and a half I had lived there lonely and brooding, and had put the last touch—the very last touch, to my work. "The Resurrection Day" went out over the world and brought me fame—and everything else that heart could desire.

[*With greater warmth*]

But I no longer loved my own work. Men's laurels and incense nauseated me, till I could have rushed away in despair and hidden myself in the depths of the woods.

[*Looking at her*]

You, who are a thought-reader—can you guess what then occurred to me?

MAIA.

[*lightly*] Yes, it occurred to you to make portrait-busts of gentlemen and ladies.

PROFESSOR RUBEK.

[*nods*] To order, yes. With animals' faces behind the masks. These I threw in gratis—into the bargain, you understand.

[*Smiling*]

But that was not precisely what I had in my mind.

MAIA.

What, then?

PROFESSOR RUBEK.

[*again serious*] It was this, that all the talk about the artist's vocation and the artist's mission, and so forth, began to strike me as being very empty, and hollow, and meaningless at bottom.

MAIA.

Then what would you put in its place?

PROFESSOR RUBEK.

Life, Maia.

MAIA.

Life?

PROFESSOR RUBEK.

Yes, is not life in sunshine and in beauty a hundred times better worth while than to hang about to the end of your days in a raw, damp hole, and wear yourself out in a perpetual struggle with lumps of clay and blocks of stone?

MAIA.

[*with a little sigh*] Yes, I have always thought so, certainly.

PROFESSOR RUBEK.

And then I had become rich enough to live in luxury and in indolent, quivering sunshine. I was able to build myself the villa on the Lake of Taunitz, and the palazzo in the capital,—and all the rest of it.

MAIA.

[*taking up his tone*] And last but not least, you could afford to treat yourself to me, too. And you gave me leave to share in all your treasures.

PROFESSOR RUBEK.

[*jesting, so as to turn the conversation*] Did I not promise to take you up with me to a high mountain and show you all the glory of the world?   ·

MAIA.

[*with a gentle expression*] You have perhaps taken me up with you to a high enough mountain, Rubek—but you have not shown me all the glory of the world.

Professor Rubek.

[*with a laugh of irritation*] How insatiable you are, Maia! Absolutely insatiable!

[*With a vehement outburst*]

But do you know what is the most hopeless thing of all, Maia? Can you guess that?

Maia.

[*with quiet defiance*] Yes, I suppose it is that you have gone and tied yourself to me—for life.

Professor Rubek.

I would not have chosen such a heartless expression.

Maia.

But that doesn't diminish the heartlessness of your meaning.

Professor Rubek.

You have no clear idea of the inner workings of an artist's nature.

MAIA.

[*smiling and shaking her head*] Good heavens, I haven't even a clear idea of the inner workings of my own nature.

PROFESSOR RUBEK.

[*continuing undisturbed*] I live at such high speed, Maia. We live so, we artists. I, for my part, have lived through a whole lifetime in the few years we two have known each other. I have come to realise that I am not at all adapted for seeking happiness in indolent enjoyment. Life does not shape *itself* that way for me and those like me. I must go on working—producing one work after another—right up to my last day.

[*Forcing himself to continue*]

That is why I cannot get on with you any longer, Maia—not with you alone.

MAIA.

[*quietly*] Does that mean, in plain language, that you have grown tired of me?

PROFESSOR RUBEK.

[*bursts forth*] Yes, that is what it means! I have

grown tired—intolerably tired and fretted and un-
strung—in this life with you! Now you know it.

[*Controlling himself*]

These are hard, ugly words I am using. I know
that very well. And you are not all to blame in this
matter;—that I willingly admit. It is simply and
solely I myself, who have once more undergone a
revolution—

[*Half to himself*]

—an awakening to my real life.

MAIA.

[*involuntarily folding her hands*] Why in all the
world should we not part then?

PROFESSOR RUBEK.

[*looks at her in astonishment*] Should you be will-
ing to?

MAIA.

[*shrugging her shoulders*] Oh yes, if there's nothing
else for it, then—

PROFESSOR RUBEK.

[*eagerly*] But there is something else for it. There
is an alternative—

MAIA.

[*holding up her forefinger*] Now you are thinking of the pale lady again!

PROFESSOR RUBEK.

Yes, to tell the truth, I cannot help constantly thinking of her. Ever since I met her again.

[*A step nearer her*]

For now I will tell you a secret, Maia.

MAIA.

Well?

PROFESSOR RUBEK.

[*touching his own breast*] In here, you see—in here I have a little bramah-locked casket. And in that casket all my sculptor's visions are stored up. But when she disappeared and left no trace, the lock of the casket snapped to. And she had the key— and she took it away with her.—You, little Maia, you had no key; so all that the casket contains must lie unused. And the years pass! And I have no means of getting at the treasure.

MAIA.

[*trying to repress a subtle smile*] Then get her to turn the key for you again—

PROFESSOR RUBEK.

[*not understanding*] Maia—?

MAIA.

—for here she *is*, you see.   And no doubt it's on account of this casket that she has come.

PROFESSOR RUBEK.

I have not said a single word to her on this subject!

MAIA.

[*looks innocently at him*] My dear Rubek—do you think it's worth while making all this fuss and commotion about so simple a matter?

PROFESSOR RUBEK.

Do you think this matter is so absolutely simple?

MAIA.

Yes, certainly I think so.   Do you attach yourself to whoever you most require.

[*Nods to him*]

I shall always manage to find a place for myself.

PROFESSOR RUBEK.

Where do you mean?

MAIA.

[*unconcerned, evasively*] Well—I need only take myself off to the villa, if it should be necessary. But it won't be; for in town—in all our great house—there must surely, with a little good will, be room enough for three.

PROFESSOR RUBEK.

[*uncertainly*] And do you think that would work in the long run?

MAIA.

[*in a light tone*] Very well, then—if it won't work, it won't. It is no good talking about it.

PROFESSOR RUBEK.

And what shall we do then, Maia—if it does not work?

MAIA.

[*untroubled*] Then we two will simply get out of each other's way—part entirely. I shall always find something new for myself, here or there in the world. Something free! Free! Free!—No need to be anxious about that, Professor Rubek!

[*Suddenly points off to the right*]

Look there! There we have her.

PROFESSOR RUBEK.

[*turning*] Where?

MAIA.

Out on the plain. Striding—like a marble statue. She is coming this way.

PROFESSOR RUBEK.

[*stands gazing with his hand over his eyes*] Does not she look like the Resurrection incarnate?

[*To himself*]

And her I could displace—and move into the shade! Remodel her—. Fool that I was!

MAIA.

What do you mean by that?

PROFESSOR RUBEK.

[*putting the question aside*] Nothing. Nothing that you would understand.

> [IRENE *advances from the right over the upland.
> The children at their play have already
> caught sight of her and run to meet her. She
> is now surrounded by them; some appear
> confident and at ease, others uneasy and*

timid. She talks low to them and indicates
that they are to go down to the hotel; she
herself will rest a little beside the brook.
The children run down over the slope to the
left, half way to the back. IRENE *goes up to*
the wall of rock, and lets the rillets of the
cascade flow over her hands, cooling them.]

MAIA.

[*in a low voice*] Go down and speak to her alone,
Rubek.

PROFESSOR RUBEK.

And where will you go in the meantime?

MAIA.

[*looking significantly at him*] Henceforth I shall
go my own ways.

[*She descends from the hillock and leaps over*
the brook, by aid of her alpenstock. She
stops beside IRENE.]

MAIA.

Professor Rubek is up there, waiting for you,
madam.

IRENE.

What does he want?

MAIA.

He wants you to help him in opening a casket, the lock of which has snapped to.

IRENE.

Can I help him there?

MAIA.

He says you are the only person that can.

IRENE.

Then I must try.

MAIA.

You must indeed, madam.

[*She goes down by the path to the hotel.*]

[*In a little while* PROFESSOR RUBEK *comes down to* IRENE, *but stops with the brook between them.*]

IRENE.

[*after a short pause*] She—the other one—said that you had been waiting for me.

PROFESSOR RUBEK.

I have waited for you year after year—without myself knowing it.

IRENE.

I could not come to you, Arnold. I was lying down there, sleeping the long, deep, dreamful sleep

PROFESSOR RUBEK.

But now you have awakened, Irene!

IRENE.

[*shakes her head*] I have the heavy, deep sleep still in my eyes.

PROFESSOR RUBEK.

You shall see that day will dawn and lighten for us both.

IRENE.

Do not believe that.

PROFESSOR RUBEK.

[*urgently*] I do believe it! And I know it Now that I have found you again—

IRENE.

Risen from the grave.

PROFESSOR RUBEK.

Transfigured!

G

IRENE.

Only risen, Arnold.   Not transfigured.

[*He crosses over to her by means of stepping-
stones below the cascade.*]

PROFESSOR RUBEK.

Where have you been all day, Irene?

IRENE.

[*pointing*] Far, far over there, on the great dead
waste—

PROFESSOR RUBEK.

[*turning the conversation*] You have not your—
your friend with you to-day, I see.

IRENE.

[*smiling*] My friend is keeping a close watch on
me, none the less.

PROFESSOR RUBEK.

Can she?

IRENE.

[*glancing furtively around*] You may be sure she
can—wherever I may go.   She never loses sight of
me—

·   [*Whispering*]

Until one fine sunny morning, I shall kill her.

PROFESSOR RUBEK.

Would you do that?

IRENE.

With the utmost delight—if only I could manage it. '

PROFESSOR RUBEK.

Why do you want to?

IRENE.

Because she deals in witchcraft.

· [*Mysteriously*]

Only think, Arnold—she has changed herself into my shadow.

PROFESSOR RUBEK.

[*trying to calm her*] Well, well, well—a shadow we must all have.

IRENE.

I am my own shadow.

[*With an outburst*]

Do you not understand that!

PROFESSOR RUBEK.

[*sadly*] Yes, yes, Irene, I understand it.

[*He seats himself on a stone beside the brook. She stands behind him, leaning against the wall of rock.*]

IRENE.

[*after a pause*] Why do you sit there turning your eyes away from me?

PROFESSOR RUBEK.

[*softly, shaking his head*] I dare not—I dare not look at you.

IRENE.

Why do you no longer dare look at me?

PROFESSOR RUBEK.

You have a shadow that tortures me. And I have the crushing weight of my conscience.

IRENE.

[*with a glad cry of deliverance*] At last!

PROFESSOR RUBEK.

[*jumps up*] Irene—what is it!

IRENE.

[*motioning him off*] Keep still, still, still!

    [*Draws a deep breath and says, as though relieved
       of a burden*]

There! Now they let me go. For this time.— Now we can sit down and talk as we used to—when I was alive.

PROFESSOR RUBEK.

Oh, if only we could talk as we used to.

IRENE.

Sit there, where you were sitting.   I will sit here beside you.

[*He sits down again.   She seats herself on another stone, close to him.*]

IRENE.

[*after a short interval of silence*] Now I have come back to you from the uttermost regions, Arnold.

PROFESSOR RUBEK.

Aye, truly, from an endless journey.

IRENE.

Come home to my lord and master—

PROFESSOR RUBEK.

To our home ;—to our own home, Irene.

IRENE.

Have you looked for me every single day?

PROFESSOR RUBEK.

How dared I look for you?

IRENE.

[*with a sidelong glance*] No, I suppose you dared not. For you understood nothing.

PROFESSOR RUBEK.

Was it really not for the sake of some one else that you all of a sudden disappeared from me in that way?

IRENE.

Might it not quite well be for your sake, Arnold?

PROFESSOR RUBEK.

[*looks doubtfully at her*] I don't understand you—?

IRENE.

When I had served you with my soul and with my body—when the statue stood there finished—our child as you called it—then I laid at your feet the most precious sacrifice of all—by effacing myself for all time.

PROFESSOR RUBEK.

[*bows his head*] And laying my life waste.

IRENE.

[*suddenly firing up*] It was just that I wanted! Never, never should you create anything again—after you had created that only child of ours.

PROFESSOR RUBEK.

Was it jealousy that moved you, then?

IRENE.

[*coldly*] I think it was rather hatred.

PROFESSOR RUBEK.

Hatred? Hatred for me?

IRENE.

[*again vehemently*] Yes, for you—for the artist who had so lightly and carelessly taken a warm-blooded body, a young human life, and worn the soul out of it—because you needed it for a work of art.

PROFESSOR RUBEK.

And you can say that—you who threw yourself into my work with such saint-like passion and such ardent joy?—that work for which we two met together every morning, as for an act of worship.

IRENE.

[*coldly, as before*] I will tell you one thing, Arnold.

PROFESSOR RUBEK.

Well?

IRENE.

I never loved your art, before I met you.—Nor after either.

PROFESSOR RUBEK.

But the artist, Irene?

IRENE.

The artist I hate.

PROFESSOR RUBEK.

The artist in me too?

IRENE.

In you most of all. When I unclothed myself and stood for you, then I hated you, Arnold—

PROFESSOR RUBEK.

[*warmly*] That you did not, Irene! That is not true!

IRENE.

I hated you, because you could stand there so unmoved—

PROFESSOR RUBEK.

[*laughs*] Unmoved? Do you think so?

IRENE.

—at any rate so intolerably self-controlled. And because you were an artist and an artist only—not a man!

[*Changing to a tone full of warmth and feeling*]

But that statue in the wet, living clay, that I loved—as it rose up, a vital human creature, out of those raw, shapeless masses — for that was our creation, our child. Mine and yours.

PROFESSOR RUBEK.

[*sadly*] It was so in spirit and in truth.

IRENE.

Let me tell you, Arnold—it is for the sake of this child of ours that I have undertaken this long pilgrimage.

PROFESSOR RUBEK.

[*suddenly alert*] For the statue's— ?

IRENE.

Call it what you will, I call it our child.

PROFESSOR RUBEK.

And now you want to see it? Finished? In marble, which you always thought so cold?

[*Eagerly*]

You do not know, perhaps, that it is installed in a great museum somewhere—far out in the world?

IRENE.

I have heard a sort of legend about it.

PROFESSOR RUBEK.

And museums were always a horror to you. You called them grave-vaults—

IRENE.

I will make a pilgrimage to the place where my soul and my child's soul lie buried.

PROFESSOR RUBEK.

[*uneasy and alarmed*] You must never see that statue again! Do you hear, Irene! I implore you—! Never, never see it again!

IRENE.

Perhaps you think it would mean death to me a second time?

PROFESSOR RUBEK.

[*clenching his hands together*] Oh I don't know what I think.—But how could I ever imagine that you would fix your mind so immovably on that statue? You, who went away from me—before it was completed.

IRENE.

It was completed. That was why I could go away from you—and leave you alone.

PROFESSOR RUBEK.

[*sits with his elbows upon his knees rocking his head from side to side, with his hands before his eyes*] It was not what it afterwards became.

IRENE.

[*quietly but quick as lightning, half-unsheathes a narrow-bladed sharp knife which she carries in her breast, and asks in a hoarse whisper*] Arnold—have you done any evil to our child?

PROFESSOR RUBEK.

[*evasively*] Any evil?—How can I be sure what you would call it?

IRENE.

[*breathless*] Tell me at once what you have done to the child!

PROFESSOR RUBEK.

I will tell you if you will sit and listen quietly to what I say.

IRENE.

[*hides the knife*] I will listen as quietly as a mother can when she—

PROFESSOR RUBEK.

[*interrupting*] And you must not look at me while I am telling you.

IRENE.

[*moves to a stone behind his back*] I will sit here, behind you.—Now tell me.

PROFESSOR RUBEK.

[*takes his hands from before his eyes and gazes straight in front of him*] When I had found you, I knew at once how I should make use of you for my life-work.

IRENE.

"The Resurrection Day" you called your life-work.—I call it "our child."

PROFESSOR RUBEK.

I was young then—with no experience of life. The Resurrection, I thought, would be most beautifully and exquisitely figured as a young unsullied woman—with none of a life's experiences—awakening to light and glory without having to put away from her anything ugly and impure.

IRENE.

[*quickly*] Yes—and so I stand there now, in our work?

PROFESSOR RUBEK.

[*hesitating*] Not absolutely and entirely so, Irene.

IRENE.

[*in rising excitement*] Not absolutely—? Do I not stand as I always stood for you?

PROFESSOR RUBEK.

[*without answering*] I learned worldly wisdom in the years that followed, Irene. "The Resurrection Day" became in my mind's eye something more and something—something more complex. The little round pedestal on which your figure stood erect and solitary—it no longer afforded room for all the imagery I now wanted to add—

IRENE.

[*gropes for her knife, but desists*] What imagery did you add then? Tell me!

PROFESSOR RUBEK.

I imaged that which I saw with my eyes around me in the world. I had to include it—I could not help it, Irene. I expanded the pedestal—made it wide and spacious. And on it I placed a segment of the curving, bursting earth. And up from the fissures of the soil there now swarm men and women with dimly-suggested animal-faces. Women and men —as I knew them in real life.

IRENE.

[*in breathless suspense*] But in the middle of the rout there stands the young woman radiant with joy of light?—Do I not stand so, Arnold?

PROFESSOR RUBEK.

[*evasively*] Not quite in the middle. I had unfortunately to move that figure a little back. For the sake of the general effect, you understand. Otherwise it would have dominated the whole too much.

IRENE.

But the joy in the light still transfigures my face?

PROFESSOR RUBEK.

Yes, it does, Irene—in a way. A little subdued perhaps—as my altered idea required.

IRENE.

[*rising noiselessly*] That design expresses the life you now see, Arnold.

PROFESSOR RUBEK.

Yes, I suppose it does.

IRENE.

And in that design you have shifted me back, a little toned down—to serve as a background-figure—in a group.

[*She draws the knife.*]

PROFESSOR RUBEK.

Not a background-figure. Let us say, at most, a figure not quite in the foreground—or something of that sort.

IRENE.

[*whispers hoarsely*] There you uttered your own doom

[*On the point of striking.*]

PROFESSOR RUBEK.

[*turns and looks at her*] Doom?

IRENE.

[*hastily hides the knife, and says as though choked with agony*] My whole soul—you and I—we, we, we and our child were in that solitary figure.

PROFESSOR RUBEK.

[*eagerly, taking off his hat and drying the drops of sweat upon his brow*] Yes, but let me tell you, too, how I have placed myself in the group. In front, beside a fountain—as it were here—sits a man weighed down with guilt, who cannot quite free himself from the earth-crust. I call him remorse for a ruined life. He sits there and dips his fingers in the purling stream—to wash them clean—and he is gnawed and tortured by the thought that never, never will he succeed. Never in all eternity will he attain to freedom and the new life. He will remain for ever prisoned in his hell.

IRENE.

[*hardly and coldly*] Poet!

PROFESSOR RUBEK.

Why poet?

IRENE.

Because you are nerveless and sluggish and full of forgiveness for all the sins of your life, in thought and in act. You have killed my soul—so you model yourself in remorse, and self-accusation, and penance—

[*Smiling*]

—and with that you think your account is cleared.

PROFESSOR RUBEK.

[*defiantly*] I am an artist, Irene, and I take no shame to myself for the frailties that perhaps cling to me. For I was born to be an artist, you see. And, do what I may, I shall never be anything else.

IRENE.

[*looks at him with a lurking evil smile, and says gently and softly*] You are a poet, Arnold.

[*Softly strokes his hair*]

You dear, great, middle-aged child,—that you cannot see that!

PROFESSOR RUBEK.

[*annoyed*] Why do you keep on calling me a poet?

IRENE.

[*with malign eyes*] Because there is something apologetic in the word, my friend. Something that suggests forgiveness of sins—and spreads a cloak over all frailty.

[*With a sudden change of tone*]

But *I* was a human being—then. And I, too, had a life to live,—and a human destiny to fulfil. And all that, look you, I let slip—gave it all up in order to make myself your bondwoman. Oh, it was a suicide—a deadly sin against myself!

[*Half whispering*]

And that sin I can never expiate !

[*She seats herself near him beside the brook, keeps close, though unnoticed, watch upon him, and as though in absence of mind, plucks some flowers from the shrubs around them.*]

IRENE.

[*with apparent self-control*] I should have borne children into the world—many children—real children —not such children as are hidden away in grave-vaults. That was my vocation. I ought never to have served you—poet.

PROFESSOR RUBEK.

[*lost in recollection*] Yet those were beautiful days
Irene.   Marvellously beautiful days—as I now look
back upon them—

IRENE.

[*looking at him with a soft expression*] Can you
remember a little word that you said—when you had
finished—finished with me and with our child?
[*Nods to him*] Can you remember that little word,
Arnold?

PROFESSOR RUBEK.

[*looks inquiringly at her*] Did I say a little word
then, which you still remember?

IRENE.

Yes, you did.   Can you not recall it?

PROFESSOR RUBEK.

[*shaking his head*] No, I can't say that I do.   Not
at the present moment, at any rate.

IRENE.

You took both my hands and pressed them warmly.
And I stood there in breathless expectation.   And
then you said: " Well now, Irene, I thank you from
my heart.   This," you said, " has been a priceless
episode for me."

PROFESSOR RUBEK.

[*looks doubtfully at her*] Did I say " episode "?   It is not a word I am in the habit of using.

IRENE.

You said " episode."

PROFESSOR RUBEK.

[*with assumed cheerfulness*] Well, well—after all, it was in reálity an episode.

IRENE.

[*curtly*] At that word I left you.

PROFESSOR RUBEK.

You take everything so painfully to heart, Irene.

IRENE.

[*drawing her hand over her forehead*] Perhaps you are right.   Let us shake off all the hard things that go to the heart.

[*Plucks off the leaves of a mountain rose and strews them on the brook*]

Look   there,   Arnold.   There   are   our   birds swimming.

PROFESSOR RUBEK.

What birds are they?

IRENE.

Can you not see? Of course they are flamingoes.
Are they not rose-red?

PROFESSOR RUBEK.

Flamingoes do not swim. They only wade.

IRENE.

Then they are not flamingoes. They are sea-gulls.

PROFESSOR RUBEK.

They may be sea-gulls with red bills, yes.

[*Plucks broad green leaves and throws them into
the brook*]

Now I send out my ships after them.

IRENE.

But there must be no harpoon-men on board.

PROFESSOR RUBEK.

No, there shall be no harpoon-men.

[*Smiles to her*]

Can you remember the summer when we used to
sit like this outside the little peasant hut on the
Lake of Taunitz?

IRENE.

[*nods*] On Saturday evenings, yes,—when we had finished our week's work—

PROFESSOR RUBEK.

—And taken the train out to the lake—to stay there over Sunday—

IRENE.

[*with an evil gleam of hatred in her eyes*] It was an episode, Arnold.

PROFESSOR RUBEK.

[*as if not hearing*] Then, too, you used to set birds swimming in the brook. They were water-lilies which you—

IRENE.

They were white swans.

PROFESSOR RUBEK.

I meant swans, yes. And I remember that I fastened a great rough leaf to one of the swans. It looked like a burdock-leaf—

IRENE.

And then it turned into Lohengrin's boat—with the swan yoked to *it*.

PROFESSOR RUBEK.

How fond you were of that game, Irene.

IRENE.

We played it over and over again.

PROFESSOR RUBEK.

Every single Saturday, I believe,—all the summer through.

IRENE.

You said I was the swan that drew your boat.

PROFESSOR RUBEK.

Did I say so? Yes, I daresay I did.

[*Absorbed in the game*]

Just see how the sea-gulls are swimming down the stream!

IRENE.

[*laughing*] And all your ships have run ashore.

PROFESSOR RUBEK.

[*throwing more leaves into the brook*] I have ships enough in reserve.

[*Follows the leaves with his eyes, throws more into the brook, and says after a pause*]

Irene,—I have bought the little peasant hut beside the Lake of Taunitz.

Irene.

Have you bought it ? You often said you would,
if you could afford it.

Professor Rubek.

The day came when I could afford it easily enough ;
and so I bought it.

Irene.

[*with a sidelong look at him*] Then do you live out
there now—in our old house ?

Professor Rubek.

No, I have had it pulled down long ago. And
I have built myself a great, handsome, comfortable
villa on the site—with a park around it. It is there
that we—

[*Stops and corrects himself*]

—there that I usually live during the summer.

Irene.

[*mastering herself*] So you and—and the other one
live out there now ?

Professor Rubek.

[*with a touch of defiance*] Yes. When my wife and
I are not travelling—as we are this year.

IRENE.

[*looking far before her*] Life was beautiful, beautiful by the Lake of Taunitz.

PROFESSOR RUBEK.

[*as though looking back into himself*] And yet, Irene—

IRENE.

[*completing his thought*] —Yet we two let slip all that life and its beauty.

PROFESSOR RUBEK.

[*softly, urgently*] Does repentance come too late, now?

IRENE.

[*does not answer, but sits silent for a moment; then she points over the upland*] Look there, Arnold,—now the sun is going down behind the peaks. See what a red glow the level rays cast over all the heathery knolls out yonder.

PROFESSOR RUBEK.

[*looks where she is pointing*] It is long since I have seen a sunset in the mountains.

IRENE.

Or a sunrise?

PROFESSOR RUBEK.

A sunrise I don't think I have ever seen.

IRENE.

[*smiles as though lost in recollection*] I once saw a marvellously lovely sunrise.

PROFESSOR RUBEK.

Did you? Where was that?

IRENE.

High, high up on a dizzy mountain-top. You beguiled me up there by promising that I should see all the glory of the world if only I—

[*She stops suddenly*]

PROFESSOR RUBEK.

If only you— ? Well?

IRENE.

I did as you told me—went with you up to the heights. And there I fell upon my knees, and worshipped you, and served you.

[*Is silent for a moment ; then says softly*]

Then I saw the sunrise.

PROFESSOR RUBEK.

[*turning the conversation*] Should you not like to come and live with us in the villa down there?

IRENE.

[*looks at him with a scornful smile*] With you— and the other woman?

PROFESSOR RUBEK.

[*urgently*] With me—as in our days of creation. You could open all that is locked up in me. Can you not find it in your heart, Irene?

IRENE.

[*shaking her head*] I have no longer the key to you, Arnold.

PROFESSOR RUBEK.

You have the key! You and you alone have it. [*Beseechingly*] Help me—that I may be able to live my life over again!

IRENE.

[*immovable as before*] Empty dreams! Idle— dead dreams. For our life there is no resurrection.

PROFESSOR RUBEK.

[*curtly, breaking off*] Then let us go on playing!

IRENE.

Yes, playing, playing—only playing!

[*They sit and strew leaves and petals over the brook, where they float and sail away.*]

[*Up the slope to the left at the back come* ULFHEIM *and* MAIA *in hunting costume. After them comes the* SERVANT *with the leash of dogs, with which he goes out to the right.*]

PROFESSOR RUBEK.

[*catching sight of them*] Ah! there is little Maia, going out with the bear-hunter.

IRENE.

Your lady, yes.

PROFESSOR RUBEK.

Or the other's.

MAIA.

[*looks around as she is crossing the upland, sees the two sitting by the brook, and calls out*] Good-night, Professor! Dream of me. Now I᾽am going off on my adventures!

PROFESSOR RUBEK.

[*calls back to her*] What is to be the object of this adventure?

MAIA.

[*approaching*] I am going to put life in the place of all the rest.

PROFESSOR RUBEK.

[*mockingly*] Aha! so you are going to do that too, little Maia?

MAIA.

Yes. And I've made a verse about it, and this is how it goes:

[*Sings triumphantly*]

I am free! I am free! I am free!
No more life in the prison for me!
I am free as a bird! I am free!

For I believe I have awakened now—at last.

PROFESSOR RUBEK.

It almost seems so—

MAIA.

[*drawing a deep breath*] Oh, how divinely light one feels on waking!

PROFESSOR RUBEK.

Good-night, Frau Maia—and good luck to—

ULFHEIM.

[*calls out, interposing*] Hush, hush!—for the devil's sake let's have none of your wizard wishes. Don't you see that we are going out to shoot—

PROFESSOR RUBEK.

What will you bring me home from the hunting, Maia?

MAIA.

You shall have a bird of prey to model. I shall wing one for you.

PROFESSOR RUBEK.

[*laughs mockingly and bitterly*] Yes, to wing things —without knowing what you are doing—has long been quite in your way.

MAIA.

[*tossing her head*] Oh, just let me look after myself for the future, and then—!

[*Nods and laughs roguishly*]

Good-bye—and a good, peaceful summer night on the upland!

PROFESSOR RUBEK.

[*jestingly*] Thanks! and all the ill-luck in the world over you and your hunting!

ULFHEIM.

[*roaring with laughter*] There now, that is a wish worth having!

MAIA.

[*laughing*] Thanks, thanks, thanks, Professor!

[*They have both crossed the visible portion of the upland, and go out through the bushes to the right.*]

PROFESSOR RUBEK.

[*after a short pause*] A summer night on the upland! Yes, that would have been life!

IRENE.

[*suddenly, with a wild expression in her eyes*] Will you have a summer night on the upland—with me?

PROFESSOR RUBEK.

[*stretching his arms wide*] Yes, yes,—come!

IRENE.

My adored lord and master!

PROFESSOR RUBEK.

Oh, Irene!

IRENE.

[*hoarsely, smiling and groping in her breast*] It will be only an episode—

[*Quickly, whispering*]

Hush!—do not look round, Arnold!

PROFESSOR RUBEK.

[*also in a low voice*] What is it?

IRENE.

A face that is staring at me.

PROFESSOR RUBEK.

[*turns involuntarily*] Where? [*With a start*] Ah—!···

| [*The* SISTER OF MERCY'S *head is partly visible among the bushes beside the descent to the left. Her eyes are immovably fixed on* IRENE.]

IRENE.

[*rises and says softly*] We must part then. No, you must remain sitting. Do you hear? You must not go with me.

[*Bends over him and whispers*]

Till we meet again—to-night—on the upland.

PROFESSOR RUBER.

And you will come, Irene?

IRENE.

Yes, certainly I will come. Wait for me here.

PROFESSOR RUBEK.

[*repeats dreamily*] Summer night on the upland. With you. With you.

[*His eyes meet hers*]

Oh, Irene—that might have been our life.—And that we have forfeited—we two.

IRENE.

We see the irretrievable only when—

[*Breaks short off*]

PROFESSOR RUBEK.

[*looks inquiringly at her*] When— ?

IRENE.

When we dead awaken.

PROFESSOR RUBEK.

[*shakes his head mournfully*] What do we really see then ?

IRENE.

We see that we have never lived.

[*She goes towards the slope and descends*]

[*The* SISTER OF MERCY *makes way for her and follows her.* PROFESSOR RUBEK *remains sitting motionless beside the brook.*]

MAIA.

[*is heard singing triumphantly among the hills*]

I am free ! I am free ! I am free !
No more life in the prison for me !
I am free as a bird ! I am free !

THIRD ACT

[*A wild riven mountain-side, with sheer precipices at the back. Snow-clad peaks rise to the right, and lose themselves in drifting mists. To the left, on a stone-scree, stands an old, half-ruined hut. It is early morning. Dawn is breaking. The sun has not yet risen.*]

[MAIA *comes, flushed and irritated, down over the stone-scree on the left.* ULFHEIM *follows, half angry, half laughing, holding her fast by the sleeve.*]

MAIA.

[*trying to tear herself loose*] Let me go! Let me go, I say!

ULFHEIM.

Come, come! are you going to bite now? You're as snappish as a wolf.

MAIA.

[*striking him over the hand*] Let me go, I tell you ?
And be quiet !

ULFHEIM.

No, confound me if I will !

MAIA.

Then I will not go another step with you.   Do
you hear ?—not a single step !

ULFHEIM.

Ho, ho !   How can you get away from me, here,
on the wild mountain-side ?

MAIA.

I will jump over the precipice yonder, if need be——

ULFHEIM.

And mangle and mash yourself up into dogs'-
meat !   A juicy morsel !

[*Lets go his hold*]

As you please.   Jump over the precipice if you
want to.   It's a dizzy drop.   There's only one
narrow footpath down it, and that's almost im-
passable.

MAIA.

[*dusts her skirt with her hand, and looks at him with angry eyes*] Well, you are a nice one to go hunting with!

ULFHEIM.

Say rather, sporting.

MAIA.

Oh! So you call this sport, do you?

ULFHEIM.

Yes, I venture to take that liberty. It is the sort of sport I like best of all.

MAIA.

[*tossing her head*] Well—I must say!

    [*After a pause ; looks searchingly at him*]

Why did you let the dogs loose up there?

ULFHEIM.

[*blinking his eyes and smiling*] So that they too might do a little hunting on their own account, don't you see?

MAIA.

There's not a word of truth in that! It wasn't
for the dogs' sake that you let them go.

ULFHEIM.

[*still smiling*] Well, why did I let them go then?
Let us hear.

MAIA.

You let them go because you wanted to get rid
of Lars. He was to run after them and bring them
in again, you said. And in the meantime—. Oh,
it was a pretty way to behave!

ULFHEIM.

In the meantime?

MAIA.

[*curtly breaking off*] No matter!

ULFHEIM.

[*in a confidential tone*] Lars won't find them. You
may safely swear to that. He won't come with them
before the time's up.

MAIA.

[*looking angrily at him*] No, I daresay not.

ULFHEIM.

[*catching at her arm*] For Lars—he knows my—
my methods of sport, you see.

MAIA.

[*eludes him and measures him with a glance*] Do
you know what you look like, Mr. Ulfheim?

ULFHEIM.

I should think I'm probably most like myself.

MAIA.

Yes, there you're exactly right. For you're the
living image of a <u>faun</u>.

ULFHEIM.

A faun?

MAIA.

Yes, precisely; a faun.

ULFHEIM.

A faun! Isn't that a sort of monster? Or a
kind of a wood demon, as you might call it?

MAIA.

Yes, just the sort of creature you are. A thing with a goat's beard and goat-legs. Yes, and the faun has horns too!

ULFHEIM.

So, so!—has h e horns too?

MAIA.

A pair of ugly horns, just like yours, yes.

ULFHEIM.

Can you see the poor little horns *I* have?

MAIA.

Yes I seem to see them quite plainly.

ULFHEIM.

[*taking the dogs' leash out of his pocket*] Then I had better see about tying you.

MAIA.

Have you gone quite mad? Would you tie me?

ULFHEIM.

If I am a demon, let me be a demon! So that's the way of *it*! You can see the horns, can you?

MAIA.

[*soothingly*] There, there, there! Now try to behave nicely, Mr. Ulfheim.

[*Breaking off*]

But what has become of that hunting-castle of yours, that you boasted so much of? You said it lay somewhere hereabouts.

ULFHEIM.

[*points with a flourish to the hut*] There you have it, before your very eyes.

MAIA.

[*looks at him*] That old pig-stye!

ULFHEIM.

[*laughing in his beard*] It has harboured more than one king's daughter, I can tell you.

MAIA.

Was it there that that horrid man you told me about came to the king's daughter in the form of a bear?

ULFHEIM.

Yes, my fair companion of the chase—this is the scene.

[*With a gesture of invitation*]

If you would deign to enter—

MAIA.

Isch! If ever I set foot in it—! Isch!

ULFHEIM.

Oh, two people can doze away a summer night in there comfortably enough. Or a whole summer, if it comes to that!

MAIA.

Thanks! One would need to have a pretty strong taste for that kind of thing.

[*Impatiently*]

But now I am tired both of you and the hunting expedition. Now I am going down to the hotel—before people awaken down there.

ULFHEIM.

How do you propose to get down from here?

MAIA.

That's your affair. There must be a way down somewhere or other, I suppose.

ULFHEIM.

[*pointing towards the back*] Oh, certainly! There is a sort of way—right down the face of the precipice yonder—

MAIA.

There, you see. With a little goodwill—

ULFHEIM.

—but just you try if you dare go that way.

MAIA.

[*doubtfully*] Do you think I can't?

ULFHEIM.

Never in this world—if you don't let me help you.

MAIA.

[*uneasily*] Why, then come and help me! What else are you here for?

ULFHEIM.

Would you rather I should take you on my back—?

MAIA.

Nonsense!

ULFHEIM.

—or carry you in my arms?

MAIA.

Now do stop talking that rubbish!

ULFHEIM.

[*with suppressed exasperation*] I once took a young girl—lifted her up from the mire of the streets and carried her in my arms. Next my heart I carried her. So I would have borne her all through life —lest haply she should dash her foot against a stone. For her shoes were worn very thin when I found her—

MAIA.

And yet you took her up and carried her next your heart?

ULFHEIM.

Took her up out of the gutter and carried her as high and as carefully as I could.

[*With a growling laugh*]

And do you know what I got for my reward?

MAIA.

No. What did you get?

ULFHEIM.

[*looks at her, smiles and nods*] I got the horns! The horns that you can see so plainly. Is not that a comical story, madam bear-murderess?

MAIA.

Oh yes, comical enough! But I know another story that is still more comical.

ULFHEIM.

How does that story go?

MAIA.

This is how it goes. There was once a stupid girl, who had both a father and a mother—but a rather poverty-stricken home. Then there came a high and mighty seigneur into the midst of all this poverty. And he took the girl in his arms—as you did—and travelled far, far away with her—

ULFHEIM.

Was she so anxious to be with him?

MAIA.

Yes, for she was stupid, you see.

ULFHEIM.

And he, no doubt, was a brilliant and beautiful personage?

MAIA.

Oh no, he wasn't so superlatively beautiful either. But he pretended that he would take her with him to the top of the highest of mountains, where there was light and sunshine without end.

ULFHEIM.

So he was a mountaineer, was he, that man?

MAIA.

Yes he was—in his way.

ULFHEIM.

And then he took the girl up with him—?

MAIA.

[*with a toss of the head*] Took her up with him finely, you may be sure! Oh no! he beguiled her into a cold, clammy cage, where—as it seemed to her—there was neither sunlight nor fresh air, but only gilding and great petrified ghosts of people all round the walls.

ULFHEIM.

Devil take me, but it served her right!

MAIA.

Yes, but don't you think it's quite a comical story, all the same?

ULFHEIM.

[*looks at her a moment*] Now listen to me, my good companion of the chase—

MAIA.

Well, what is it now?

ULFHEIM.

Should not we two tack our poor shreds of life together?

MAIA.

Is his worship inclined to set up as a patching-tailor?

ULFHEIM.

Yes, indeed he is. Might not we two try to draw the rags together here and there—so as to make some sort of a human life out of them?

MAIA.

And when the poor tatters were quite worn out—
what then?

ULFHEIM.

[*with a large gesture*] Then there we shall stand
free and serene—as the man and woman we really
are!

MAIA.

[*laughing*] You with your goat-legs, yes!

ULFHEIM.

And you with your—. Well let that pass.

MAIA.

Yes, come—let us pass—on.

ULFHEIM.

Stop! Whither away, comrade?

MAIA.

Down to the hotel, of course,

ULFHEIM.

And afterwards?

MAIA.

Then we'll take a polite leave of each other, with thanks for pleasant company.

ULFHEIM.

Can we part, we two? Do you think we can?

MAIA.

Yes, you didn't manage to tie me up, you know.

ULFHEIM.

I have a castle to offer you—

MAIA.

[*pointing to the hut*] A fellow to that one?

ULFHEIM.

It has not fallen to ruin yet.

MAIA.

And all the glory of the world, perhaps?

ULFHEIM.

A castle, I tell you—

MAIA.

Thanks! I have had enough of castles.

K

ULFHEIM.

—with splendid hunting-grounds stretching for miles around it.

MAIA.

Are there works of art too in this castle?

ULFHEIM.

[*slowly*] Well, no—it's true there are no works of art; but—

MAIA.

[*relieved*] Ah! that's one good thing, at any rate!

ULFHEIM.

Will you go with me, then—as far and as long as I want you.

MAIA.

There is a tame bird of prey keeping watch upon me.

ULFHEIM.

[*wildly*] We'll put a bullet in his wing, Maia!

MAIA.

[*looks at him a moment, and says resolutely*] Come then, and carry me down into the depths.

ULFHEIM.

[*puts his arm round her waist*] It is high time!
The mist is upon us!

MAIA.

Is the way down terribly dangerous?

ULFHEIM.

The mountain mist is more dangerous still.

[*She shakes him off, goes to the edge of the preci-*
pice and looks over, but starts quickly back.]

ULFHEIM

[*goes towards her, laughing*] What? Does it make
you a little giddy?

MAIA.

[*faintly*] Yes, that too. But go and look over.
Those two, coming up—

ULFHEIM.

[*goes and bends over the edge of the precipice*] It's
only your bird of prey—and his strange lady.

MAIA.

Can't we get past them—without their seeing us?

ULFHEIM.

Impossible! The path is far too narrow. And there's no other way down.

MAIA.

[*nerving herself*] Well, well — let us face them here, then!

ULFHEIM.

Spoken like a true bear-killer, comrade!

[PROFESSOR RUBEK *and* IRENE *appear over the edge of the precipice at the back. He has his plaid over his shoulders; she has a fur cloak thrown loosely over her white dress, and a swansdown hood over her head.*]

PROFESSOR RUBEK.

[*still only half visible above the edge*] What, Maia! So we two meet once again?

MAIA.

[*with assumed coolness*] At your service. Won't you come up?

[PROFESSOR RUBEK *climbs right up and holds out his hand to* IRENE, *who also comes right to the top.*]

·PROFESSOR RUBEK.

[*coldly to* MAIA] So you, too, have been all night
on the mountain,—as we have?

MAIA.

I have been hunting—yes. You gave me permission, you know.

ULFHEIM.

[*pointing downward*] Have you come up that path
there?

PROFESSOR RUBEK.

As you saw.

ULFHEIM.

And the strange lady too?

PROFESSOR RUBEK.

Yes, of course.

[*With a glance at* MAIA]

Henceforth the strange lady and I do not intend
our ways to part.

ULFHEIM.

Don't you know, then, that it is a deadly dangerous
way you have come?

PROFESSOR RUBEK.

We thought we would try, nevertheless. For it did not seem particularly hard at first.

ULFHEIM.

No, at first nothing seems hard. But presently you may come to a tight place where you can neither get forward nor back. And then you stick fast, Professor! Mountain-fast, as we hunters call it.

PROFESSOR RUBEK.

[*smiles and looks at him*] Am I to take these as oracular utterances, Mr. Ulfheim?

ULFHEIM.

Lord preserve me from playing the oracle!

[*Urgently, pointing up towards the heights*]

But don't you see that the storm is upon us? Don't you hear the blasts of wind?

PROFESSOR RUBEK.

[*listening*] They sound like the prelude to the Resurrection Day.

ULFHEIM.

They are storm-blasts from the peaks, man! Just

look how the clouds are rolling and sinking—soon
they'll be all around us like a winding-sheet!

IRENE.

[*with a start and shiver*] I know that sheet!

MAIA.

[*drawing* ULFHEIM *away*] Let us make haste and
get down.

ULFHEIM.

[*to* PROFESSOR RUBEK] I cannot help more than
one. Take refuge in the hut in the meantime—
while the storm lasts. Then I shall send people up
to fetch the two of you away.

IRENE.

[*in terror*] To fetch us away! No, no!

ULFHEIM.

[*harshly*] To take you by force if necessary—for
it's a matter of life and death here. Now, you
know it.

[*To* MAIA]

Come, then—and don't fear to trust yourself in
your comrade's hands.

MAIA.

[*clinging to him*] Oh, how I shall rejoice and sing, if I get down with a whole skin!

ULFHEIM.

[*begins the descent and calls to the others*] You'll wait, then, in the hut, till the men come with ropes, and fetch you away.

[ULFHEIM, *with* MAIA *in his arms, clambers rapidly but warily down the precipice.*]

IRENE.

[*looks for some time at* PROFESSOR RUBEK *with terror-stricken eyes*] Did you hear that, Arnold?—men are coming up to fetch me away! Many men will come up here—

PROFESSOR RUBEK.

Do not be alarmed, Irene!

IRENE.

[*in growing terror*] And she, the woman in black —she will come too. For she must have missed me long ago. And then she will seize me, Arnold! And put me in the strait-waistcoat. Oh, she has it with her, in her box. I have seen it with my own eyes—

PROFESSOR RUBEK.

Not a soul shall be suffered to touch you.

IRENE.

[*with a wild smile*] Oh no—I myself have a resource against that.

PROFESSOR RUBEK.

What resource do you mean?

IRENE.

[*drawing out the knife*] This!

PROFESSOR RUBEK.

[*tries to seize it*] Have you a knife?

IRENE.

Always, always—both day and night—in bed as well!

PROFESSOR RUBEK.

Give me that knife, Irene!

IRENE.

[*concealing it*] You shall not have it. I may very likely find a use for it myself.

PROFESSOR RUBEK.

What use can you have for it, here?

IRENE.

[*looks fixedly at him*] It was intended for you, Arnold.

PROFESSOR RUBEK.

For me!

IRENE.

As we were sitting by the Lake of Taunitz last evening—

PROFESSOR RUBEK.

By the Lake of—

IRENE.

—outside the peasant's hut—and playing with swans and water-lilies—

PROFESSOR RUBEK.

What then—what then?

IRENE.

—and when I heard you say with such deathly, icy coldness—that I was nothing but an episode in your life—

PROFESSOR RUBEK.

It was you that said that, Irene, not I

IRENE.

[*continuing*] —then I had my knife out. I wanted to stab you in the back with it.

PROFESSOR RUBEK.

[*darkly*] And why did you hold your hand?

IRENE.

Because it flashed upon me with a sudden horror that you were dead already—long ago.

PROFESSOR RUBEK.

Dead?

IRENE.

Dead. Dead, you as well as I. We sat there by the Lake of Taunitz, we two clay-cold bodies— and played with each other.

PROFESSOR RUBEK.

I do not call that being dead. But you do not understand me.

IRENE.

Then where is the burning desire for me that you fought and battled against when I stood freely forth before you as the woman arisen from the dead?

PROFESSOR RUBEK.

Our love is assuredly not dead, Irene.

IRENE.

The love that belongs to the life of earth—the beautiful, miraculous life of earth—the inscrutable life of earth—that is dead in both of us.

PROFESSOR RUBEK.

[*passionately*] And do you know that just that love—it is burning and seething in me as hotly as ever before?

IRENE.

And I? Have you forgotten who I now am?

PROFESSOR RUBEK.

Be who or what you please, for aught I care! For me, you are the woman I see in my dreams of you.

IRENE.

I have stood on the turn-table—naked—and made a show of myself to many hundreds of men—after you.

PROFESSOR RUBEK.

It was I that drove you to the turn-table—blind

as I then was—I, who placed the dead clay-image
above the happiness of life—of love.

IRENE.

[*looking down*] Too late—too late!

PROFESSOR RUBEK.

Not by a hairsbreadth has all that has passed in
the interval lowered you in my eyes.

IRENE.

[*with head erect*] Nor in my own!

PROFESSOR RUBEK.

Well, what then! Then we are free—and there
is still time for us to live our life, Irene.

IRENE.

[*looks sadly at him*] The desire for life is dead
in me, Arnold. Now I have arisen. And I look for
you. And I find you.—And then I see that you
and life lie dead—as I have lain.

PROFESSOR RUBEK.

Oh, how utterly you are astray! Both in us and

around us life is fermenting and throbbing as fiercely as ever!

IRENE.

[*smiling and shaking her head*] The young woman of your Resurrection Day can see all life lying on its bier.

PROFESSOR RUBEK.

[*throwing his arms violently around her*] Then let two of the dead—us two—for once live life to its uttermost—before we go down to our graves again!

IRENE.

[*with a shriek*] Arnold!

PROFESSOR RUBEK.

But not here in the half darkness! Not here with this hideous dank shroud flapping around us—

IRENE.

[*carried away by passion*] Nò, no—up in the light, and in all the glittering glory! Up to the Peak of Promise!

PROFESSOR RUBEK.

There we will hold our marriage-feast, Irene—oh, my beloved!

IRENE.

[*proudly*] The sun may freely look on us, Arnold.

PROFESSOR RUBEK.

All the powers of light may freely look on us— and all the powers of darkness too.

[*Seizes her hand*]

Will you then follow me, oh my grace-given bride?

IRENE.

[*as though transfigured*] I follow you, freely and gladly, my lord and master!

PROFESSOR RUBEK

[*drawing her along with him*] We must first pass through the mists, Irene, and then—

IRENE.

Yes, through all the mists, and then right up to the summit of the tower that shines in the sunrise.

[*The mist-clouds close in over the scene*—PRO-FESSOR RUBEK *and* IRENE, *hand in hand, climb up over the snow-field to the right and soon disappear among the lower clouds. Keen storm-gusts hurtle and whistle through the air.*]

[*The* SISTER OF MERCY *appears upon the stone-scree to the left. She stops and looks around silently and searchingly.*]

[MAIA *can be heard singing triumphantly far in the depths below.*]

MAIA.

I am free! I am free! I am free!
No more life in the prison for me!
I am free as a bird! I am free!

[*Suddenly a sound like thunder is heard from high up on the snow-field, which glides and whirls downwards with rushing speed.* PROFESSOR RUBEK *and* IRENE *can be dimly discerned as they are whirled along with the masses of snow and buried in them.*]

THE SISTER OF MERCY.

[*gives a shriek, stretches out her arms towards them and cries*] Irene!

[*Stands silent a moment, then makes the sign of the cross before her in the air, and says*]

Pax vobiscum!

[MAIA'S *triumphant song sounds from still farther down below.*]

Printed by BALLANTYNE, HANSON & Co.
Edinburgh & London

CATALOGUE   MCM

21 BEDFORD STREET, W.C.

Telegrams, *Sunlocks, London*

Telephone, *2279, Gerrard*

The Books mentioned in this List can be obtained to order by any Bookseller if not in stock, or will be sent by the Publisher on receipt of the published price and postage.

Art and Decoration.

THE LIFE AND DEATH OF MR. BADMAN. Presented to the world in a familiar dialogue between MR. WISEMAN and MR. ATTENTIVE. By JOHN BUNYAN, Author of "The Pilgrim's Progress." With Twelve Compositions by GEORGE WOOLLISCROFT RHEAD and LOUIS RHEAD designed to portray the deadly sins of the ungodly Mr. Badman's journey from this world to Hell. One Volume quarto on Imitation hand-made paper. Price 15s. net.

₊ *Also a limited edition on Dutch Hand-made Paper at £1 11s. 6d. net*

THE SQUARE BOOK OF ANIMALS. By WILLIAM NICHOLSON. With Rhymes by ARTHUR WAUGH. The Popular Edition, lithographed on Cartridge-paper. 4to boards. Price 5s.

Also a limited edition, on Japanese vellum. Price 12s. 6d. net.

LONDON TYPES. By WILLIAM NICHOLSON. Twelve Coloured Plates, each illustrating a type. With Quatorzains by W. E. HENLEY. 4to, boards. Lithographed on Cartridge Paper. Price 5s.

₊ *A few sets of the Plates, printed from the Original Woodblocks, and Hand-coloured by the Artist, in Portfolio. Price Twenty Guineas net.*

AN ALMANAC OF TWELVE SPORTS FOR 1900. By WILLIAM NICHOLSON. Twelve Coloured Plates, each illustrating a sport for the month. With accompanying Rhymes by RUDYARD KIPLING. 4to, boards. Lithographed on Cartridge Paper. Price 2s. 6d.

₊ *A few sets of the Plates, printed from the Original Woodblocks and Hand-coloured by the Artist, in Portfolio. Price Twenty Guineas net.*

AN ALPHABET. By WILLIAM NICHOLSON. Twenty-six Coloured Plates, each illustrating a letter of the alphabet. 4to, boards. Lithographed on Cartridge Paper. Price 5s.

The Library Edition (Limited). Lithographed in Colours on Dutch Hand-made Paper, mounted on brown paper and bound in cloth, Gilt Edges. Price 12s. 6d. net.

₊ *A few sets of the Plates, printed from the Original Woodblocks and Hand-coloured by the Artist, in Portfolio. Price £21 net.*

TWELVE PORTRAITS. By WILLIAM NICHOLSON—HER MAJESTY THE QUEEN, H.R.H. THE PRINCE OF WALES, THE ARCHBISHOP OF CANTERBURY, SARAH BERNHARDT, CECIL RHODES, LORD ROBERTS, JAMES McNEILL WHISTLER, PRINCE BISMARCK, SIR HENRY IRVING, W. E. GLADSTONE, RUDYARD KIPLING, SIR HENRY HAWKINS. Each portrait is lithographed in colours, and mounted on cardboard, 15 in. by 16¼ in. In Portfolio. Price 21s. net.

₊ *A few sets of the Plates have been taken from the Original Woodblocks and Hand-coloured by the Artist. Price £21 net.*

BRITISH CONTEMPORARY ARTISTS. Critical Studies of WATTS, MILLAIS, ALMA-TADEMA, BURNE-JONES, ORCHARDSON, LEIGHTON, and POYNTER. By COSMO MONKHOUSE. In One Volume, Royal 8vo. Illustrated. Price One Guinea net.

GAINSBOROUGH. And His Place in English Art. By SIR WALTER ARMSTRONG, Director of the National Gallery, Ireland. With 62 Photogravures from Photographs specially taken for this Edition, and printed on the finest French plate paper, and 10 Lithographs in Colours. In One Volume, large imperial 4to, gilt top. A reprint of 250 copies only. Price £5 5s. net.

RUBENS. His Life, his Work, and his Time. By EMILE MICHEL. Translated by ELIZABETH LEE. With 40 Coloured Plates, 40 Photogravures and 272 Text Illustrations. In Two Volumes, Imperial 8vo, £2 2s. net.

LEONARDO DA VINCI. Artist, Thinker, and Man of Science. From the French of EUGÈNE MUNTZ, Member of the Institute of France, &c. With 48 Plates and 252 Text Illustrations. In Two Volumes. Price £2 2s. net.

MEISSONIER. His Life, and His Art. By VALLERY C. O. GREARD, de l'Académie Française. Translated from the French by LADY MARY LOYD and FLORENCE SIMMONDS. With 38 full-page plates, 20 in Photogravure and 18 in Colour, and 200 Text Illustrations. Imperial 8vo, £1 16s. net.

ANTONIO ALLEGRI DA CORREGGIO: His Life, his Friends, and his Time. By CORRADO RICCI, Director of the Royal Gallery, Parma. Translated by FLORENCE SIMMONDS. With 16 Photogravure Plates, 21 full-page Plates in Tint, and 190 Illustrations in the Text. Imperial 8vo, £2 2s. net. Also in 14 parts, price 2s. 6d. each net.

. *Also a special edition printed on Japanese vellum, limited to 100 copies, with duplicate plates on India paper. Price £12 12s. net.*

REMBRANDT: His Life, his Work, and his Time. By EMILE MICHEL, Member of the Institute of France. Translated by FLORENCE SIMMONDS. Edited and Prefacd by FREDERICK WEDMORE. Second Edition, Enlarged, with 76 full-page Plates, and 250 Illustrations in the Text. In One Volume, gilt top, or in Two Volumes, imperial 8vo, £2 2s. net.

. *A few copies of the* EDITION DE LUXE *of the First Edition, printed on Japanese vellum with India proof duplicates of the photogravures, are still on sale, price £12 12s net.*

REMBRANDT. Seventeen of his Masterpieces from the collection of his Pictures in the Cassel Gallery. Reproduced in Photogravure by the Berlin Photographic Company. With an Essay by FREDERICK WEDMORE. In large portfolio 27½ inches × 20 inches.

The first twenty-five impressions of each plate are numbered and signed, and of these only fourteen are for sale in England at the net price of Twenty Guineas *the set. The price of the impressions after the first twenty-five is* Twelve Guineas *net, per set.*

FASHION IN PARIS. The various Phases of Feminine Taste and Æsthetics from 1797 to 1897. By OCTAVE UZANNE. From the French by Lady MARY LOYD. With 100 Hand-coloured Plates and 250 Text Illustrations by FRANÇOIS COURBOIN. In One Volume, imperial 8vo. Price 36s.

A HISTORY OF DANCING: From the Earliest Ages to Our Own Times. From the French of GASTON VUILLIER. With 24 Plates in Photogravure and 409 Illustrations in the Text. In One Volume, 4to. Price, cloth, 36s. net, or Vellum, gilt top 50s. net.

. *Also 35 copies printed on Japanese vellum (containing 3 additional Plates), with a duplicate set of the Plates on India paper for framing. Each copy numbered and signed, price £12 12s. net.*

MASTERPIECES OF GREEK SCULPTURE. A Series of Essays on the History of Art. By ADOLF FURTWANGLER. Authorised Translation. Edited by EUGENIE SELLERS. With 19 full page and 200 text Illustrations. Imperial 8vo, £3 3s. net.

. *Also an* EDITION DE LUXE *on Japanese vellum, limited to 50 numbered s in Two Volumes* 12 12s *net.*

with the Ceiling of the Hall where they were originally painted. By MARY E. WILLIAMS. Folio, cloth, £2 2s. net.

BEAUTY AND ART. By ALDAM HEATON. Crown 8vo, cloth, 6s.

CATALOGUE OF THE EXHIBITION OF INTER- NATIONAL ART, KNIGHTSBRIDGE, 1898. THE INTER-NATIONAL SOCIETY OF SCULPTORS, PAINTERS AND GRAVERS, ILLUSTRATED SOUVENIR. In One Volume, 4to, boards. With 108 Reproductions from the works exhibited (including 3 Photogravures). Price 3s. 6d. net.

A CATALOGUE OF THE ACCADEMIA DELLE BELLE ARTI AT VENICE. With Biographical Notices of the Painters and Reproductions of some of their Works. Edited by E. M. KEARY. Crown 8vo, cloth, 2s. 6d. net ; paper, 2s. net.

A CATALOGUE OF THE MUSEO DEL PRADO AT MADRID. Compiled by E. LAWSON. Crown 8vo, cloth, 3s. net ; paper, 2s. 6d. net.

ANIMAL SYMBOLISM IN ECCLESIASTICAL ARCHITECTURE. By E. P. EVANS. With a Bibliography and Seventy-eight Illustrations, crown 8vo, 9s.

Biography, Correspondence, and History.

THE VERSAILLES HISTORICAL SERIES.

A Series of Memoirs, Correspondence, and Letters of Noted Persons belonging to the different European Courts, giving Graphic Descriptions of Court Life, State Secrets, and the Private Sayings and Doings of Royalty and Court Attachés. Translated and arranged by KATHERINE PRESCOTT WORMELEY. *Illustrated with over Ninety Photogravures. In Eight Vols., demy 8vo, price Seven Guineas net, or separately as follows. The Edition is limited to 200 sets for Great Britain.*

MEMOIRS OF THE DUC DE SAINT-SIMON. On the Times of Louis XIV. and the Regency. Translated and arranged from the edition collated with the original manuscript by M. CHÉRUEL. Four Volumes. Price £3 13s. 6d. net.

THE PRINCE DE LIGNE. His Memoirs, Letters, and Miscellaneous Papers. With Introduction and Preface by C.-A. SAINTE-BEUVE and Madame de STAEL-HOLSTEIN. Two Volumes. 42s. net.

THE CORRESPONDENCE OF MADAME, PRIN- CESS PALATINE, Mother of the Regent; of MARIE ADELAIDE DE SAVOIE, Duchesse de Bourgogne ; and of Madame DE MAINTENON, in relation to Saint-Cyr. Preceded by Introductions from C.-A. SAINTE-BEUVE. One Volume. 21s. net.

THE BOOK OF ILLUSTRIOUS LADIES. By PIERRE DE BOURDEILLE, ABBÉ DE BRANTOME. With Elucidations on some of those Ladies by C.-A. SAINTE-BEUVE. One Volume. 21s. net.

NEW LETTERS OF NAPOLEON I. Omitted from the Edition published under the auspices of Napoleon III. Trans'ated from the French by Lady MARY LOYD. In One Volume, demy 8vo, with Frontispiece, price 15s. net.

1812. NAPOLEON I. IN RUSSIA. By VASSILI VEREST-CHAGIN. With an Introduction by R. WHITEING. Illustrated from Sketches and Paintings by the Author. Crown 8vo, 6s.

MEMOIRS OF SERGEANT BOURGOGNE (1812-1813). Authorised Translation, from the French Original edited by PAUL COTTIN and MAURICE HÉNAULT. With a Frontispiece. 8vo, cloth. Price 6s.

THE MEMOIRS OF VICTOR HUGO. With a Preface by PAUL MEURICE. Translated by JOHN W. HARDING. With a Portrait, 8vo. Price 10s. net.

THE LIFE AND LETTERS OF JOHN DONNE (DEAN OF ST. PAUL'S). Now for the first time Revised and Collected by EDMUND GOSSE, M.A. of Trinity College, Cambridge, Hon. LL.D. of the University of St. Andrews. In Two Volumes, 8vo. Price 24s. net.

THE PAGET PAPERS. Diplomatic and other Correspondence of THE RIGHT HON. SIR ARTHUR PAGET, G.C.B., 1794-1807. With two Appendices, 1808 and 1828-1829. Arranged and Edited by his son, The Right Hon. SIR AUGUSTUS B. PAGET, G.C.B., late Her Majesty's Ambassador in Vienna. With Notes by Mrs. J. R. GREEN. New Edition with Index. In Two Volumes, demy 8vo, with Portraits, 32s. net.

DE QUINCEY MEMORIALS. Being Letters and other Records here first Published, with Communications from COLERIDGE, the WORDSWORTHS, HANNAH MORE, PROFESSOR WILSON, and others. Edited with Introduction, Notes, and Narrative, by ALEXANDER H. JAPP, LL.D., F.R.S.E. In Two Volumes, demy 8vo, cloth, with Portraits, 30s. net.

LETTERS OF SAMUEL TAYLOR COLERIDGE. Edited by ERNEST HARTLEY COLERIDGE. With 16 Portraits and Illustrations. In Two Volumes, demy 8vo, £1 12s.

THE LIFE OF NELSON. By ROBERT SOUTHEY. A New Edition. Edited by DAVID HANNAY. Crown 8vo, gilt, with Portraits of Lord Nelson after HOPPNER and Lady Hamilton after ROMNEY, price 6s.

MEMOIR OF ROBERT, EARL NUGENT. With Letters, Poems, and Appendices. By CLAUD NUGENT. With reproductions from Family Portraits by Sir GODFREY KNELLER Sir JOSHUA REYNOLDS, GAINSBOROUGH, and others. In One Volume, 8vo. Pr.ce 16s.

THE LIFE OF JUDGE JEFFREYS. By H. B. IRVING, M.A. Oxon. Demy 8vo, with Three Portraits and a Facsimile, 12s. 6d. net.

MARYSIENKA: Marie de la Grange d'Arquien, Queen of Poland, and Wife of Sobieski (1641-1716). By K. WALISZEWSKI. Translated from the French by Lady MARY LOYD. In One Volume, with Portrait. 8vo, cloth. Price 12s. net.

PETER THE GREAT. By K. WALISZEWSKI, Author of "The Romance of an Empress," "The Story of a Throne." Translated from the French by Lady MARY LOYD. With a Portrait. 8vo, cloth, 6s.; or Library Edition, in Two Volumes, 8vo, 28s.

CARDINAL MANNING. From the French of FRANCIS DE PRESSENSÉ by E. INGALL. Crown 8vo, 5s.

THE PALMY DAYS OF NANCE OLDFIELD. By EDWARD ROBINS. With Portraits. 8vo, 12s. 6d.

AS OTHERS SAW HIM. A Retrospect, A.D. 54. Crown 8vo, gilt top, 6s.

BROTHER AND SISTER. A Memoir and the Letters of ERNEST and HENRIETTE RENAN. Translated by Lady MARY LOYD. Demy 8vo, with Two Portraits in Photogravure, and Four Illustrations, 14s.

CHARLES GOUNOD. Autobiographical Reminiscences with Family Letters and Notes on Music. Translated by the Hon. W. HELY HUTCHINSON. Demy 8vo, with Portrait, 10s. 6d.

MEMOIRS. By CHARLES GODFREY LELAND (HANS BREITMANN). Second Edition. 8vo, with Portrait, price 7s. 6d.

EDMOND AND JULES DE GONCOURT. Letters and Leaves from their Journals. Selected. In Two Volumes, 8vo, with Eight Portraits, 32s.

ALEXANDER III. OF RUSSIA. By CHARLES LOWE, M.A., Author of "Prince Bismarck: an Historical Biography." Crown 8vo, with Portrait in Photogravure, 6s.

PRINCE BISMARCK. An Historical Biography. By CHARLES LOWE, M.A. With Two Portraits. Cheap Edition, crown 8vo, 2s. 6d.

MY FATHER AND I. By Comtesse DE PULIGA. One Volume. Crown 8vo, price 6s.

STORY OF THE PRINCESS DES URSINS IN SPAIN. (Camarera-Mayor). By CONSTANCE HILL. With 12 Portraits and a Frontispiece. In One Volume, 8vo. Price 7s. 6d. net.

CATHERINE SFORZA. By COUNT PASOLINI. Abridged and Translated by PAUL SYLVESTER. Illustrated with numerous reproductions from Original Pictures and documents. Demy 8vo, 16s.

VILLIERS DE L'ISLE ADAM: His Life and Works. From the French of VICOMTE ROBERT DU PONTAVICE DE HEUSSEY. By Lady MARY LOYD. With Portrait and Facsimile. Crown 8vo, cloth, 10s. 6d.

THE LIFE OF HENRIK IBSEN. By HENRIK JÆGER. Translated by CLARA BELL. With the Verse done into English from the Norwegian Original by EDMUND GOSSE. Crown 8vo, cloth, 6s.

RECOLLECTIONS OF MIDDLE LIFE. By FRANCISQUE SARCEY. Translated by E. L. CAREY. 8vo, with Portrait, 10s 6d.

TWENTY-FIVE YEARS IN THE SECRET SERVICE. The Recollections of a Spy. By Major HENRI LE CARON. With New Preface. 8vo, boards, price 2s. 6d., or cloth, 3s. 6d.
  ⁎ *The Library Edition, with Portraits and Facsimiles, 8vo, 14s., is still on sale.*

STUDIES IN FRANKNESS. By CHARLES WHIBLEY. Crown 8vo, with Frontispiece, price 7s. 6d.

A BOOK OF SCOUNDRELS. By CHARLES WHIBLEY. Crown 8vo, with Frontispiece, price 7s. 6d.

THE PAGEANT OF LIFE: A Book of Dandies. By CHARLES WHIBLEY. Crown 8vo, cloth, 7s. 6d.

GREAT LIVES AND EVENTS.

Uniformly bound in cloth, 6s. each volume.

SIXTY YEARS OF EMPIRE: 1837-1897. A Review of the Period. With over 70 Portraits and Diagrams.

RECOLLECTIONS OF COUNT LEO TOLSTOY. Together with a Letter to the Women of France on the "Kreutzer Sonata." By C. A. Fehrs. Translated from the Russian by C. E. Turner, English Lecturer in the University of St. Petersburg. With Portrait.

THE FAMILY LIFE OF HEINRICH HEINE. Illustrated by one hundred and twenty-two hitherto unpublished letters addressed by him to different members of his family. Edited by his nephew, Baron Ludwig von Embden, and translated by Charles Godfrey Leland. With 4 Portraits.

THE NATURALIST OF THE SEA-SHORE. The Life of Philip Henry Gosse. By his son, Edmund Gosse, Hon. M.A. Trinity College, Cambridge. With a Portrait.

MEMOIRS OF THE PRINCE DE JOINVILLE. Translated from the French by Lady Mary Loyd. With 78 Illustrations from drawings by the Author.

ALFRED, LORD TENNYSON. A Study of His Life and Work. By Arthur Waugh, B.A. Oxon. With Twenty Illustrations from Photographs specially taken for this Work. Five Portraits, and Facsimile of Tennyson's MS.

NAPOLEON AND THE FAIR SEX. From the French of Frédéric Masson. With a Portrait.

PETER THE GREAT. By K. Waliszewski. Translated from the French by Lady Mary Loyd. With a Portrait.

THE STORY OF A THRONE. Catherine II. of Russia. From the French of K. Waliszewski. With a Portrait.

THE ROMANCE OF AN EMPRESS. Catherine II. of Russia. From the French of K. Waliszewski. With a Portrait.

A FRIEND OF THE QUEEN. Marie Antoinette and Count Fersen. From the French of Paul Gaulot. Two Portraits.

THE WOMEN OF HOMER. By Walter Copland Perry. With numerous Illustrations, large crown 8vo, 6s.

THE LOVE LETTERS OF MR. H. AND MISS R. 1775-1779. Edited by Gilbert Burgess. Square crown 8vo, 5s.

LETTERS OF A BARITONE. By Francis Walker. Square crown 8vo, 5s.

LETTERS OF A COUNTRY VICAR. Translated from the French of Yves le Querdec. By M. Gordon Holmes. Crown 8vo, 5s.

half-leather, gilt top, 7s. 6d.

ISRAEL AMONG THE NATIONS. Translated from the French of ANATOLE LEROY-BEAULIEU, Member of the Institute of France. Crown 8vo, 7s. 6d.

THE JEW AT HOME. Impressions of a Summer and Autumn Spent with Him in Austria and Russia. By JOSEPH PENNELL. With Illustrations by the Author. 4to, cloth, 5s

THE NEW EXODUS. A Study of Israel in Russia. By HAROLD FREDERIC. Demy 8vo, Illustrated, 16s.

SPANISH PROTESTANTS IN THE SIXTEENTH CENTURY. Compiled from Dr. Wilken's German Work. By RACHEL CHALLICE. With an Introduction by the Most Rev. LORD PLUNKET, late Archbishop of Dublin, and a Preface by the Rev. Canon FLEMING. Crown 8vo, 4s. 6a. net.

QUEEN JOANNA I. OF NAPLES, SICILY, AND JERUSALEM ; Countess of Provence, Forcalquier, and Piedmont. An Essay on her Times. By ST. CLAIR BADDELEY. Imperial 8vo, with numerous Illustrations, 16s.

CHARLES III. OF NAPLES AND URBAN VI.; also CECCO D'ASCOLI, Poet, Astrologer, Physican. Two Historical Essays. By ST. CLAIR BADDELEY. With Illustrations, 8vo, cloth, 10s. 6d.

ROBERT THE WISE AND HIS HEIRS, 1278–1352. By ST. CLAIR BADDELEY. 8vo, 21s.

MY PARIS NOTE-BOOK. By ALBERT D. VANDAM, Author of "An Englishman in Paris." Demy 8vo, price 6s.

UNDERCURRENTS OF THE SECOND EMPIRE. By ALBERT D. VANDAM. Demy 8vo, cloth, 7s. 6d. net.

STUDIES IN DIPLOMACY. By Count BENEDETTI, French Ambassador at the Court of Berlin. Demy 8vo, with a Portrait, 10s. 6d.

AN AMBASSADOR OF THE VANQUISHED. Viscount Elie De Gontaut-Biron's Mission to Berlin, 1871–1877. From his Diaries and Memoranda. By the DUKE DE BROGLIE. Translated with Notes by ALBERT D. VANDAM. In One Volume, 8vo, 10s. 6d.

A HISTORY OF THE LIVERPOOL PRIVATEERS, and Letters of Marque; with an account of the Liverpool Slave Trade. By GOMER WILLIAMS. In One Volume, demy 8vo, price 12s. net.

THE CASTLES OF ENGLAND : their Story and Structure, By Sir JAMES D. MACKENZIE, Bart. Dedicated by gracious permission to H.M. the Queen. In Two Volumes, Imperial 8vo, with 40 full-page Plates, and over 150 Illustrations in the Text and many Plans. Price £3 3s. net.

KRUPP'S STEEL WORKS. By FRIEDRICH C. G. MÜLLER. With 88 Illustrations by FELIX SCHMIDT and ANDERS MONTAN. Authorised Translation from the German. 4to. Price 25s. net.

THE LITTLE MANX NATION. (Lectures delivered at the Royal Institution, 1891.) By HALL CAINE, Author of "The Bondman," "The Scapegoat," &c. Crown 8vo, cloth, 3s. 6d.; paper, 2s. 6d.

DENMARK : its History, Topography, Language, Literature. Fine Arts, Social Life, and Finance. Edited by H. WEITEMEYER. Demy 8vo, cloth, with Map, 12s. 6d.
. *Dedicated, by permission, to H.R.H. the Princess of Wales.*

THE REALM OF THE HABSBURGS. By SIDNEY WHITMAN, Author of "Imperial Germany." Crown 8vo, 7s. 6d.

IMPERIAL GERMANY. A Critical Study of Fact and Character. By SIDNEY WHITMAN. New Edition, Revised and Enlarged. Crown 8vo, cloth, 2s. 6d.; paper, 2s.

THE GENESIS OF THE UNITED STATES. A Narrative of the Movement in England, 1605–1616, which resulted in the Plantation of North America by Englishmen, disclosing the Contest between England and Spain for the Possession of the Soil now occupied by the United States of America; set forth through a series of Historical Manuscripts now first printed, together with a Re-issue of Rare Contemporaneous Tracts, accompanied by Bibliographical Memoranda, Notes, and Brief Biographies. Collected, Arranged, and Edited by ALEXANDER BROWN, F.R.H.S. With 100 Portraits, Maps, and Plans. In Two Volumes, royal 8vo, buckram, £3 13s. 6d. net.

THE TRANSVAAL FROM WITHIN. A Private Record of Public Affairs. By J. P. FITZPATRICK. 8vo, cloth, 10s. net.

Travel and Adventure.

IN THE FORBIDDEN LAND. An Account of a Journey in Tibet; Capture by the Tibetan Authorities; Imprisonment, Torture, and Ultimate Release. By A. HENRY SAVAGE LANDOR, Author of "Corea, the Land of the Morning Calm," &c. Also various Official Documents, including the Enquiry and Report by J. LARKIN, Esq., Appointed by the Government of India. With a Map and 250 Illustrations. Popular Edition in one volume. Large 8vo. Price 7s. 6d. net.

COREA, OR CHO-SEN, THE LAND OF THE MORN-ING CALM. By A. HENRY SAVAGE LANDOR. With 38 Illustrations from Drawings by the Author, and a Portrait, demy 8vo, 18s.

THE INDIAN FRONTIER WAR. Being an Account of the Mohmund and Tirah Expeditions, 1897. By LIONEL JAMES, Special Correspondent for Reuter's Agency and Artist for the *Graphic*. With 32 full-page Illustrations from Drawings by the Author, and Photographs, and 10 Plans and Maps. 8vo, price 7s. 6d.

THE CHITRAL CAMPAIGN. A Narrative of Events in Chitral, Swat, and Bajour. By H. C. THOMSON. With over 50 Illustrations reproduced from Photographs, and important Diagrams and Map. Second Edition, demy 8vo, 14s. net.

WITH THE ZHOB FIELD FORCE, 1890. By Captain CRAWFORD McFALL, K.O.Y.L.I. Demy 8vo, with Illustrations, 18s.

ROMANTIC INDIA. By ANDRÉ CHEVRILLON. Translated from the French by WILLIAM MARCHANT. 8vo, 7s. 6d. net

UNDER THE DRAGON FLAG. My Experiences in the Chino-Japanese War. By JAMES ALLAN. Crown 8vo, 2s.

UNDER QUEEN AND KHEDIVE. The Autobiography of an Anglo-Egyptian Official. By Sir W. F. MIÉVILLE, K.C.M.G. Crown 8vo, with Portrait, price 6s.

UNDER THE AFRICAN SUN. A Description of Native Races in Uganda. Sporting Adventures and other Experiences. By W. J. ANSORGE, M.A., LL.D., M.R.C.S., L.R.C.P., late Senior Professor at the Royal College of Mauritius, Medical Officer to Her Majesty's Government in Uganda. With 134 Illustrations from Photographs by the Author and Two Coloured Plates. Royal 8vo. Price 21s. net.

MOGREB-EL-ACKSA. A Journey in Morocco. By R. B. CUNNINGHAME GRAHAM. With a Portrait and Map. In One Volume,

TIMBUCTOO THE MYSTERIOUS. By Felix Dubois. Translated from the French by Diana White. With 153 Illustrations from Photographs and Drawings made on the spot, and Eleven Maps and Plans. Demy 8vo, 12s. 6d.

RHODESIA PAST AND PRESENT. By S. J. Du Toit. In One Volume, 8vo, with Sixteen full-page Illustrations, 7s. 6d.

THE NEW AFRICA. A Journey up the Chobé and down the Okovanga Rivers. By Aurel Schulz, M.D., and August Hammar, C.E. In One Volume, demy 8vo, with Illustrations, 28s.

ACTUAL AFRICA ; or, The Coming Continent. A Tour of Exploration. By Frank Vincent, Author of "The Land of the White Elephant." With Map and over 100 Illustrations, demy 8vo, cloth, price 24s.

TWELVE MONTHS IN KLONDIKE. By Robert C. Kirk. With 100 Illustrations and a Map. Crown 8vo, cloth. 6s. net.

THE CUBAN AND PORTO-RICAN CAMPAIGNS. By Richard Harding Davis, F.R.G S. With 119 Illustrations from Photographs and Drawings on the Spot, and Maps. Crown 8vo, cloth, 7s. 6d. net.

CUBA IN WARTIME. By Richard Harding Davis, Author of "Soldiers of Fortune." With numerous Illustrations by Frederic Remington. Crown 8vo, price 3s. 6d.

MY FOURTH TOUR IN WESTERN AUSTRALIA. By Albert F. Calvert, F.R.G.S. 4to, with many Illustrations and Photographs, price 21s. net.

THE LAND OF THE MUSKEG. By H. Somers Somerset. Second Edition. Demy 8vo, with Maps and over 100 Illustrations, 280 pp., 14s. net.

THE OUTGOING TURK. Impressions of a Journey through the Western Balkans. By H. C. Thomson, Author of "The Chitral Campaign." Demy 8vo, with Illustrations from Original Photographs. Price 14s. net.

NOTES FOR THE NILE. Together with a Metrical Rendering of the Hymns of Ancient Egypt and of the Precepts of Ptah-hotep (the oldest book in the world). By Hardwicke D. Rawnsley, M.A. Imperial 16mo, cloth, 5s.

TEN DAYS AT MONTE CARLO AT THE BANK'S EXPENSE. Containing Hints to Visitors and a General Guide to the Neighbourhood. By V. B. Fcap. 8vo, 2s.

IN THE TRACK OF THE SUN. Readings from the Diary of a Globe-Trotter. By Frederick Diodati Thompson. With many Illustrations by Mr. Harry Fenn and from Photographs. 4to, 25s.

THE WORKERS. An Experiment in Reality. By Walter A. Wyckoff. The East. With Five Illustrations, crown 8vo. Price 3s. net.

THE WORKERS. An Experiment in Reality. By Walter A Wyckoff. The West. With Twelve Illustrations, crown 8vo. Price 3s. net.

*** *The Two Volumes in Card Box*, 6s. net.

THE QUEEN'S SERVICE. Being the Experiences of a Private Soldier in the British Infantry at Home and Abroad. By Horace Wyndham, late of the —th Regt. 3s. 6d.

TROOPER 3809. A Private Soldier of the Third Republic. By Lionel Decle, Author of "Three Years in Savage Africa." With

THE CANADIAN GUIDE-BOOK. Part I. The Tourist's
and Sportsman's Guide to Eastern Canada and Newfoundland, including full
descriptions of Routes, Cities, Points of Interest, Summer Resorts, Fishing
Places, &c., in Eastern Ontario, The Muskoka District, The St. Lawrence
Region, The Lake St. John Country, The Maritime Provinces, Prince
Edward Island, and Newfoundland. With an Appendix giving Fish and
Game Laws, and Official Lists of Trout and Salmon Rivers and their
Lessees. By CHARLES G. D. ROBERTS, Professor of English Literature in
King's College, Windsor, N.S. With Maps and many Illustrations.
Crown 8vo, limp cloth, 6s.

THE CANADIAN GUIDE-BOOK. Part II. WESTERN
CANADA. Including the Peninsula and Northern Regions of Ontario,
the Canadian Shores of the Great Lakes, the Lake of the Woods Region,
Manitoba and "The Great North-West," The Canadian Rocky Mountains
and National Park, British Columbia, and Vancouver Island. By ERNEST
INGERSOLL. With Maps and many Illustrations. Crown 8vo, limp cloth, 6s.

THE GUIDE-BOOK TO ALASKA AND THE NORTH-
WEST COAST, including the Shores of Washington, British Columbia
South-Eastern Alaska, the Aleutian and the Sea Islands, the Behring
and the Arctic Coasts. By E. R. SCIDMORE. With Maps and many
Illustrations. Crown 8vo, limp cloth, 6s.

Essays and Belles Lettres, &c.

WILLIAM SHAKESPEARE. A Critical Study. By
GEORGE BRANDES, Ph.D. Translated from the Danish by WILLIAM
ARCHER, DIANA WHITE, and MARY MORISON. Students' Edition. In
One Volume, demy 8vo, buckram uncut, 10s. net.

HENRIK IBSEN. BJÖRNSTJERNE BJÖRNSON.
Critical Studies. By GEORGE BRANDES. Authorised Translation from
the Danish. With Introductions by WILLIAM ARCHER. In One Volume,
demy 8vo. Roxburgh, gilt top, or buckram, uncut. 10s. net.

THE SYMBOLIST MOVEMENT IN LITERATURE.
By ARTHUR SYMONS. Crown 8vo, buckram, 6s.

SEVENTEENTH-CENTURY STUDIES. A Contribu
tion to the History of English Poetry. By EDMUND GOSSE, Clark
Lecturer on English Literature at the University of Cambridge; Hon.
M.A. of Trinity College, Cambridge. A New Edition. Crown 8vo,
buckram, gilt top, 7s. 6d.

CRITICAL KIT-KATS. By EDMUND GOSSE. Crown 8vo,
buckram, gilt top, 7s 6d.

QUESTIONS AT ISSUE. Essays. By EDMUND GOSSE.
Crown 8vo, buckram, gilt top, 7s. 6d.
     ** A Limited Edition on Large Paper, 25s. net.

GOSSIP IN A LIBRARY. By EDMUND GOSSE. Third
Edition. Crown 8vo, buckram, gilt top, 7s. 6d.
     ** A Limited Edition on Large Paper, 25s. net.

CORRECTED IMPRESSIONS. Essays on Victorian Writers.
By GEORGE SAINTSBURY. Crown 8vo, gilt top, 7s. 6d.

ESSAYS. By ARTHUR CHRISTOPHER BENSON, of Eton College. Crown 8vo, buckram, 7s 6d.

A COMMENTARY ON THE WORKS OF HENRIK
IBSEN. By HJALMAR HJORTH BOYESEN. Crown 8vo, cloth, 7s. 6d. net.

THE POSTHUMOUS WORKS OF THOMAS DE
QUINCEY. Edited, with Introduction and Notes from the Author's Original MSS., by ALEXANDER H. JAPP, LL.D., F.R.S.E., &c. Crown 8vo, cloth, 6s. each.

I. SUSPIRIA DE PROFUNDIS. With other Essays.

II. CONVERSATION AND COLERIDGE. With other Essays.

THE WORKS OF LORD BYRON. Edited by WILLIAM
ERNEST HENLEY. To be completed in Twelve Volumes. (The Letters, Diaries, Controversies, Speeches, &c., in Four, and the Verse in Eight.) Small crown 8vo, price 5s. net each.

VOL. I.—LETTERS, 1804-1813. With a Portrait after PHILLIPS.

VOL. V.—VERSE VOLUME I. Containing "Hours of Idleness," "English Bards and Scotch Reviewers," and "Childe Harold." With a Portrait by HOLMES. [In preparation.

THE PROSE WORKS OF HEINRICH HEINE.
Translated by CHARLES GODFREY LELAND, M.A., F.R L.S. (HANS BREITMANN). In Eight Volumes.

The Library Edition, in crown 8vo, cloth, at 5s per Volume. Each Volume of this edition is sold separately. The Cabinet Edition, in special binding boxed, price £2 10s. the set. The Large Paper Edition, limited to 50 Numbered Copies, price 15s. per Volume net, will only be supplied to subscribers for the Complete Work.

I. FLORENTINE NIGHTS, SCHNABELEWOPSKI, THE RABBI OF BACHARACH, and SHAKE-SPEARE'S MAIDENS AND WOMEN.

II., III. PICTURES OF TRAVEL. 1823-1828.

IV. THE SALON. Letters on Art, Music, Popular Life, and Politics.

V., VI. GERMANY.

VII., VIII. FRENCH AFFAIRS. Letters from Paris 1832, and Lutetia.

THE COMING TERROR. And other Essays and Letters.
By ROBERT BUCHANAN. Second Edition. Demy 8vo, cloth, 12s. 6d.

THE GENTLE ART OF MAKING ENEMIES. As
pleasingly exemplified in many instances, wherein the serious ones of this earth, carefully exasperated, have been prettily spurred on to indiscretions and unseemliness, while overcome by an undue sense of right. By J. M'NEILL WHISTLER. *A New Edition.*
[In preparation.

AMERICA AND THE AMERICANS. From a French Point of View. In one volume. Crown 8vo, 3s. 6d.

"MADE IN GERMANY." Reprinted with Additions from *The New Review*. By ERNEST E. WILLIAMS. Crown 8vo, cloth, 2s. 6d. Also Popular Edition, paper covers, 1s.

THE FOREIGNER IN THE FARMYARD. By ERNEST E. WILLIAMS, Author of "Made in Germany." Crown 8vo, 2s. 6d.

MR. FROUDE AND CARLYLE. By DAVID WILSON. In One Volume, 8vo, 10s. 6d.

CAN WE DISARM? By JOSEPH McCABE. Written in Collaboration with GEORGES DARIEN. Crown 8vo, cloth, 2s. 6d.

THE LABOUR MOVEMENT IN AMERICA. By RICHARD T. ELY, Ph.D., Associate in Political Economy, Johns Hopkins University. Crown 8vo, cloth, 5s.

PARADOXES. By MAX NORDAU, Author of "Degeneration," "Conventional Lies of our Civilisation," &c. Translated by J. R. McILRAITH. With an Introduction by the Author written for this Edition. Demy 8vo, 17s. net.

CONVENTIONAL LIES OF OUR CIVILIZATION. By MAX NORDAU, Author of "Degeneration." Second English Edition. Demy 8vo, 17s. net.

DEGENERATION. By MAX NORDAU. Ninth English Edition. Demy 8vo, 17s. net. Also, a Popular Edition. 8vo, 6s.

GENIUS AND DEGENERATION: A Psychological Study. By Dr. WILLIAM HIRSCH. Translated from the Second German Edition. Demy 8vo, 17s. net.

THE NON-RELIGION OF THE FUTURE. From the French of MARIE JEAN GUYAU. In One Volume, demy 8vo, 17s. net.

STUDIES OF RELIGIOUS HISTORY. By ERNEST RENAN, late of the French Academy. 8vo, 7s. 6d.

THE SPINSTER'S SCRIP. As Compiled by CECIL RAYNOR. Narrow crown 8vo, limp cloth, 2s. 6d.

THE PINERO BIRTHDAY BOOK. Selected and arranged by MYRA HAMILTON. With a Portrait. 16mo, cloth, 2s. 6d.

THE POCKET IBSEN. A Collection of some of the Master's best known Dramas, condensed, revised, and slightly rearranged for the benefit of the Earnest Student. By F. ANSTEY, Author of "Vice Versa," "Voces Populi," &c. With Illustrations reproduced, by permission, from *Punch*, and a new Frontispiece by BERNARD PARTRIDGE. New Edition. 16mo, cloth, 3s. 6d.; or paper, 2s. 6d.

WOMAN—THROUGH A MAN'S EYEGLASS. By MALCOLM C. SALAMAN. With Illustrations by DUDLEY HARDY. Crown 8vo, cloth, 3s. 6d. ; or picture boards, 2s.

STORIES OF GOLF. Collected by WILLIAM KNIGHT and T. T. OLIPHANT. With Rhymes on Golf by various hands ; also Shakespeare on Golf, &c. *Enlarged Edition.* Fcap. 8vo, cloth, 2s. 6d.

THE ROSE : A Treatise on the Cultivation, History, Family Characteristics, &c., of the various Groups of Roses. With Accurate Description of the Varieties now Generally Grown. By H. B. ELLWANGER. With an Introduction by GEORGE H. ELLWANGER. 12mo, cloth, 5s.

THE GARDEN'S STORY ; or, Pleasures and Trials of an Amateur Gardener. By G. H. ELLWANGER. With an Introduction by the Rev. C. WOLLEY DOD. 12mo, cloth, with Illustrations, 5s.

GIRLS AND WOMEN. By E. CHESTER. Pot 8vo, cloth, 2s. 6d., or gilt extra, 3s. 6d.

THE COMPLETE INDIAN HOUSEKEEPER AND COOK. Giving the Duties of Mistress and Servants, the General Management of the House, and Practical Recipes for Cooking in all its Branches. By FLORA ANNIE STEEL and GRACE GARLINER. Fourth Edition, revised to date. Crown 8vo. Price 6s.

DRIVING FOR PLEASURE ; or, The Harness Stable and its Appointments. By FRANCIS T. UNDERHILL. Illustrated with One Hundred and Twenty-four full page Plates. Imperial 8vo, buckram sides, leather back, price 28s. net.

MANNERS, CUSTOMS, AND OBSERVANCES : Their Origin and Signification. By LEOPOLD WAGNER. Crown 8vo, 6s.

THE GREAT WAR OF 189—. A Forecast. By Rear-Admiral COLOMB, Col. MAURICE, R.A., Captain MAUDE, ARCHIBALD FORBES, CHARLES LOWE, D. CHRISTIE MURRAY, and F. SCUDAMORE. Second Edition. In One Volume, large 8vo, with numerous Illustrations, 6s.

JOHN KING'S QUESTION CLASS. By CHARLES M. SHELDON, Author of "In His Steps," &c. Crown 8vo, paper, 2s. ; cloth, 2s. 6d.

THE PASSION PLAY AT OBERAMMERGAU, 1890. By F. W. FARRAR, D.D., F.R.S., Dean of Canterbury, &c. &c. 4to, cloth, 2s. 6d.

THE WORD OF THE LORD UPON THE WATERS. Sermons read by His Imperial Majesty the Emperor of Germany, while at Sea on his Voyages to the Land of the Midnight Sun. Composed by Dr. RICHTER, Army Chaplain, and Translated from the German by JOHN R. McILRAITH. 4to, cloth, 2s. 6d.

THE KINGDOM OF GOD IS WITHIN YOU. Christianity not as a Mystic Religion but as a New Theory of Life. By

Dramatic Literature.

CYRANO DE BERGERAC. A Play in Five Acts. By EDMOND ROSTAND. Translated from the French by GLADYS THOMAS and MARY F. GUILLEMARD. Small 4to, 5s. Also, Popular Edition, 16mo, cloth, 2s. 6d.; paper, 1s. 6d.

THE PLAYS OF W. E. HENLEY AND R. L. STEVEN-SON. Crown 8vo, cloth. An Edition of 250 copies only, 10s. 6d. net, or separately, 16mo, cloth, 2s. 6d. each, or paper, 1s. 6d.
  DEACON BRODIE. | ADMIRAL GUINEA.
  BEAU AUSTIN. | MACAIRE.

THE PLAYS OF ARTHUR W. PINERO. Paper covers, 1s. 6d.; or cloth, 2s. 6d. each.
  THE TIMES. | THE AMAZONS.
  THE PROFLIGATE. | THE NOTORIOUS MRS. EBB-
  THE CABINET MINISTER | SMITH.
  THE HOBBY HORSE. | THE BENEFIT OF THE
  LADY BOUNTIFUL. | DOUBT.
  THE MAGISTRATE. | THE PRINCESS AND THE
  DANDY DICK. | BUTTERFLY.
  SWEET LAVENDER. | TRELAWNY OF THE
  THE SCHOOL-MISTRESS. | "WELLS."
  THE WEAKER SEX. |
  * THE SECOND MRS. TANQUERAY.

* This play can be had in Library form, 4to, cloth. With a Portrait of the Author. 5s.

THE PLAYS OF HENRIK IBSEN. Small 4to, cloth, 5s. each, or paper covers, 1s. 6d each.
  JOHN GABRIEL BORKMAN. | *THE MASTER BUILDER.
  LITTLE EYOLF. | *HEDDA GABLER.
  * Also a Limited Large Paper Edition, 21s. net.

BRAND: A Dramatic Poem in Five Acts. By HENRIK IBSEN. Translated in the original metres, with an Introduction and Notes, by C. H. HERFORD. Small 4to, cloth, 7s. 6d.

THE PLAYS OF GERHART HAUPTMANN.
  THE SUNKEN BELL. Fcap. 8vo, boards, 5s.
  HANNELE. Small 4to, with Portrait, 5s. Paper covers, 1s. 6d.; or cloth, 2s. 6d.
  LONELY LIVES. Paper covers, 1s. 6d.; or cloth, 2s. 6d.
  THE WEAVERS. Paper covers, 1s. 6d.; or cloth, 2s. 6d.

THE PRINCESS MALEINE: A Drama in Five Acts (Translated by GERARD HARRY), and THE INTRUDER: A Drama in One Act. By MAURICE MAETERLINCK. With an Introduction by HALL CAINE, and a Portrait of the Author. Small 4to, cloth, 5s.

THE FRUITS OF ENLIGHTENMENT: A Comedy in Four Acts. By Count LYOF TOLSTOY. Translated from the Russian by E. J. DILLON. With Introduction by A. W. PINERO. Small 4to, with Portrait, 5s.

THE GHETTO. A Drama in Four Acts. Freely adapted from the Dutch of Herman Heijermans, Jun. by CHESTER BAILEY FERNALD. 16mo, cloth, 2s. 6d.; paper, 1s. 6d.

KING ERIK: A Tragedy. By EDMUND GOSSE. A Re-issue, with a Critical Introduction by Mr. THEODORE WATTS. Fcap. 8vo, boards, 5s. net.

HYPATIA. A Play in Four Acts. Founded on CHARLES KINGSLEY'S Novel. By G. STUART OGILVIE. With Frontispiece by J. D. BATTEN. Crown 8vo, cloth, printed in Red and Black, 2s. 6d. net.

THE DRAMA: ADDRESSES. By HENRY IRVING. With Portrait by J. McN. WHISTLER. Second Edition. Fcap. 8vo, 3s. 6d.

SOME INTERESTING FALLACIES OF THE MODERN STAGE. An Address delivered to the Playgoers' Club at St. James's Hall, on Sunday, 6th December, 1891. By HERBERT BEERBOHM TREE. Crown 8vo, sewed, 6d. net.

Poetry.

THE FOREST CHAPEL, and other Poems. By MAXWELL GRAY, Author of "The Silence of Dean Maitland," "The Last Sentence," &c. Fcap. 8vo. Price 5s.

POEMS FROM THE DIVAN OF HAFIZ. Translated from the Persian by GERTRUDE LOWTHIAN BELL. Small crown 8vo, price 6s.

THE POETRY OF WILFRID BLUNT. Selected and arranged by W. E. HENLEY and GEORGE WYNDHAM. With an Introduction by W. E. HENLEY. Crown 8vo, price 6s.

ON VIOL AND FLUTE. By EDMUND GOSSE. Fcap. 8vo, with Frontispiece and Tailpiece, price 3s. 6d. net.

FIRDAUSI IN EXILE, and other Poems. By EDMUND GOSSE. Fcap. 8vo, with Frontispiece, price 3s. 6d. net.

IN RUSSET AND SILVER. POEMS. By EDMUND GOSSE. Author of "Gossip in a Library," &c. Fcap 8vo, price 3s. 6d. net.

THE POETRY OF PATHOS AND DELIGHT. From the Works of COVENTRY PATMORE. Passages selected by ALICE MEYNELL. With a Photogravure Portrait from an Oil Painting by JOHN SARGENT, A.R.A. Fcap. 8vo, 5s.

A CENTURY OF GERMAN LYRICS. Translated from the German by KATE FREILIGRATH KROEKER. Fcap. 8vo, rough edges, 3s. 6d.

LOVE SONGS OF ENGLISH POETS, 1500–1800. With Notes by RALPH H. CAINE. Fcap. 8vo, rough edges, 3s. 6d.
   *** *Large Paper Edition, limited to* 100 *Copies,* 10s. 6d. net.

IN CAP AND GOWN. Three Centuries of Cambridge Wit. Edited by CHARLES WHIBLEY. Third Edition, with a New Introduction, and a Frontispiece, crown 8vo, 3s. 6d. net.

IVY AND PASSION FLOWER: Poems. By GERARD BENDALL, Author of "Estelle," &c. &c. 12mo, cloth, 3s. 6d.

VERSES. By GERTRUDE HALL. 12mo, cloth, 3s. 6d.

IDYLLS OF WOMANHOOD. By C. AMY DAWSON. Fcap. 8vo, gilt top, 5s.

TENNYSON'S GRAVE. By ST. CLAIR BADDELEY. 8vo,

Education and Science.
THE WORLD IN 1900.

A New Geographical Series. Edited by H. J. MACKINDER, M.A., Student of Christ Church, Reader in Geography in the University of Oxford, Principal of Reading College.

The Series will consist of Twelve Volumes, each being an essay descriptive of a great natural region, its marked physical features, and the life of its peoples. Fully Illustrated in the Text and with many Maps and Diagrams.

LIST OF THE SUBJECTS AND AUTHORS:

1. **BRITAIN AND THE NORTH ATLANTIC.** By the EDITOR. [*In the press.*

2. **SCANDINAVIA AND THE ARCTIC OCEAN.** By Sir CLEMENTS R. MARKHAM, K.C.B., F.R.S., President of the Royal Geographical Society.

3. **THE MEDITERRANEAN AND FRANCE.** By ELISÉE RECLUS, Professor of Geography in the New University of Brussels, Author of the "Nouvelle Géographie Universelle."

4. **CENTRAL EUROPE.** By Dr. JOSEPH PARTSCH, Professor of Geography in the University of Breslau.

5. **AFRICA.** By Dr. J. SCOTT KELTIE, Secretary of the Royal Geographical Society, Editor of "The Statesman's Year Book," Author of "The Partition of Africa."

6. **THE NEAR EAST.** By D. G. HOGARTH, M.A., Fellow of Magdalen College, Oxford, Director of the British School at Athens, Author of "A Wandering Scholar in the Levant."

7. **THE RUSSIAN EMPIRE.** By PRINCE KROPOTKIN, Author of the Articles "Russia," "Siberia" and "Turkestan" in the "Encyclopædia Britannica."

8. **THE FAR EAST.** By ARCHIBALD LITTLE, Author of "Through the Yang-tse Gorges."

9. **INDIA.** By Col. Sir THOMAS HOLDICH, K.C.I.E., C.B., R.E., Superintendent of Indian Frontier Surveys.

10. **AUSTRALASIA AND ANTARCTICA.** By H. O. FORBES, LL.D. Director of Museums to the Corporation of Liverpool, formerly Director of the Christchurch Museum, N.Z., Author of "A Naturalist's Wanderings in the Eastern Archipelago," "A Handbook to the Primates."

11. **NORTH AMERICA.** By ISRAEL C. RUSSELL, Professor of Geography in the University of Michigan.

THE GREAT EDUCATORS.

A Series of Volumes by Eminent Writers, presenting in their entirety " A Biographical History of Education."

Each subject forms a complete volume, crown 8vo, 5s.

ARISTOTLE, and the Ancient Educational Ideals. By THOMAS DAVIDSON, M.A., LL.D.

LOYOLA, and the Educational System of the Jesuits. By Rev. THOMAS HUGHES, S.J.

ALCUIN, and the Rise of the Christian Schools. By Professor ANDREW F. WEST, Ph.D.

FROEBEL, and Education by Self-Activity. By H. COURThofe BOWEN, M.A.

ABELARD, and the Origin and Early History of Universities. By Professor JULES GABRIEL COMPAYRÉ.

HERBART AND THE HERBARTIANS. By CHARLIS DE GARMO, Ph.D.

THOMAS AND MATTHEW ARNOLD, and their Influence on English Education. By Sir JOSHUA FITCH, M.A., LL.D.

HORACE MANN, and the Common School Revival in the United States. By B. A. HINSDALE, Ph.D., LL.D.

ROUSSEAU; and, Education according to Nature. By THOMAS DAVIDSON, M.A., LL.D.

PESTALOZZI; and the Modern Elementary School. By M. A. PINLOCHE, Professor in the University of Lille. [*In preparation.*

HEINEMANN'S SCIENTIFIC HANDBOOKS.

THE BIOLOGICAL PROBLEM OF TO-DAY: Preformation or Epigenesis? Authorised Translation from the German of Prof. Dr. OSCAR HERTWIG, of the University of Berlin. By P. CHALMERS MITCHELL, M.A, Oxon. With a Preface by the Translator. Crown 8vo. 3s. 6d.

MANUAL OF BACTERIOLOGY. By A. B. GRIFFITHS, Ph.D., F.R.S. (Edin.), F.C.S. Crown 8vo, cloth, Illustrated. 7s. 6d.

MANUAL OF ASSAYING GOLD, SILVER, COPPER, TIN, AND LEAD ORES. By WALTER LEE BROWN, B.Sc. Revised, Corrected, and considerably Enlarged, and with chapters on the Assaying of Fuels, Iron and Zinc Ores, &c. By A. B. GRIFFITHS, Ph.D., F.R.S. (Edin.), F.C.S. Crown 8vo, cloth. Illustrated, 7s. 6d.

GEODESY. By J. HOWARD GORE. Crown 8vo, cloth, Illustrated, 5s.

THE PHYSICAL PROPERTIES OF GASES. By ARTHUR L. KIMBALL, of the Johns Hopkins University. Crown 8vo, cloth, Illustrated, 5s.

TELEPHOTOGRAPHY. An Elementary Treatise on the Construction and Application of the Telephotographic Lens. By THOMAS R. DALLMEYER, F.R.A.S., Vice-President of the Royal Photographic Society. 4to, cloth, with 26 Plates and 68 Diagrams. Price, 15s. net.

OUTLINES OF THE EARTH'S HISTORY. A Popular Study in Physiography. By NATHANIEL SOUTHGATE SHALER. 8vo, with Ten full-page Illustrations. 7s 6d.

EVOLUTIONAL ETHICS AND ANIMAL PSYCH-OLOGY. By E. P. EVANS. Crown 8vo, 9s.

MOVEMENT. Translated from the French of E. MAREY. By ERIC PRITCHARD, M.A., M.B. Oxon. In One Volume, crown 8vo with 170 Illustrations, 7s. 6d.

LUMEN. By CAMILLE FLAMMARION. Authorised Translation from the French by A. A. M. and R. M. With portions of the last chapter written specially for this edition. Crown 8vo, 3s. 6d.

THE STORY OF THE GREEKS. By H. A. GUERBER. Crown 8vo, with Illustrations. 3s. 6d.

ARABIC AUTHORS: A Manual of Arabian History and Literature. By F. F. ARBUTHNOT, M.R.A.S., Author of "Early Ideas," "Persian Portraits," &c. 8vo, cloth, 5s.

THE MYSTERIES OF CHRONOLOGY. With proposal for a New English Era to be called the "Victorian." By F. F. ARBUTHNOT. 8vo, 6s. net.

THE SPEECH OF MONKEYS. By Professor R. L. GARNER. Crown 8vo, 7s. 6d

Law.

A SHORT TREATISE OF BELGIAN LAW AND LEGAL PROCEDURE. From a Practical Standpoint, for the Guidance of British Traders, Patentees, and Bankers, and British Residents in Belgium. By GASTON DE LEVAL. Fcap. 8vo, paper, 1s. 6d.

PRISONERS ON OATH, PRESENT AND FUTURE, By Sir HERBERT STEPHEN, Bart. 8vo, boards, 1s. net.

THE ARBITRATOR'S MANUAL. Under the London Chamber of Arbitration. Being a Practical Treatise on the Power and Duties of an Arbitrator, with the Rules and Procedure of the Court of Arbitration, and the Forms. By JOSEPH SEYMOUR SALAMAN, Author of "Trade Marks," &c. Fcap. 8vo, 3s. 6d.

Juvenile.

MOTHER DUCK'S CHILDREN. A Coloured Picture Book by "GUGU" (The Countess RASPONI). With Verses for Young and Old. In quarto boards. Price 5s.

IN THE DEEP WOODS. 'Possum Stories. B ALBERT

Fiction.

BOULE DE SUIF. From the French of GUY DE MAUPAS-
SANT. With an Introduction by ARTHUR SYMONS, and 56 Wood
Engravings from Drawings by F. THÉVENOT. Royal 8vo, boards. 500
copies only, on Japanese vellum. 15s. net.

Popular 6s. Novels.

BENEFITS FORGOT. By WOLCOTT BALESTIER.

A CHAMPION IN THE SEVENTIES. By EDITH A.
BARNETT.

A DAUGHTER OF THIS WORLD. By F. BATTER-
SHALL.

EQUALITY. By EDWARD BELLAMY, Author of "Looking
Backward."

MAMMON & CO. By E. F. BENSON, Author of "Dodo."

THE AMAZING LADY. By M. BOWLES.

THE BROOM OF THE WAR-GOD. By II. N. BRAILS-
FORD.

A SUPERFLUOUS WOMAN. By EMMA BROOKE.

TRANSITION. By the Author of "A Superfluous Woman."

LIFE THE ACCUSER. By the Author of "A Superfluous
Woman."

THE CHRISTIAN. By HALL CAINE.

THE MANXMAN. By HALL CAINE.

THE BONDMAN. A New Saga. By HALL CAINE.

THE SCAPEGOAT. By HALL CAINE.

THE LAKE OF WINE. By BERNARD CAPES.

COTTAGE FOLK. By Mrs. COMYNS CARR.

JASPAR TRISTRAM. By A. W. CLARKE.

THE NIGGER OF THE "NARCISSUS." By JOSEPH
CONRAD.

LAST STUDIES. By HUBERT CRACKANTHORPE. With an
Introduction by Mr. HENRY JAMES, and a Portrait.

SENTIMENTAL STUDIES. By HUBERT CRACKANTHORPE.

ACTIVE SERVICE. By STEPHEN CRANE.

THE THIRD VIOLET. By STEPHEN CRANE.

THE OPEN BOAT. By STEPHEN CRANE.

PICTURES OF WAR. (The Red Badge of Courage, The
Little Regiment, &c.). By STEPHEN CRANE.

Fiction.—Popular 6s. Novels.

THE CHILD OF PLEASURE. By GABRIELE D'ANNUNZIO.

THE VICTIM. By GABRIELE D'ANNUNZIO.

THE TRIUMPH OF *DEATH*. By GABRIELE D'ANNUNZIO.

THE VIRGINS OF THE ROCKS. By GABRIELE D'ANNUNZIO.

THE LION AND THE UNICORN AND OTHER STORIES. By RICHARD HARDING DAVIS. Illustrated.

SOLDIERS OF FORTUNE. By RICHARD HARDING DAVIS.

GOD'S FOUNDLING. By A. J. DAWSON.

HEARTS IMPORTUNATE. By EVELYN DICKINSON.

THE IMAGE BREAKERS. By GERTRUDE DIX.

THE STORY OF A MODERN WOMAN. By ELLA HEPWORTH DIXON.

FOLLY CORNER. By Mrs. HENRY DUDENEY.

THE MATERNITY OF HARRIOTT WICKEN. By MRS. HENRY DUDENEY.

CHINATOWN STORIES. By CHESTER BAILEY FERNALD.

GLORIA MUNDI. By HAROLD FREDERIC.

ILLUMINATION. By HAROLD FREDERIC.

THE MARKET PLACE. By HAROLD FREDERIC.

PHASES OF AN INFERIOR PLANET. By ELLEN GLASGOW.

THE BETH BOOK. By SARAH GRAND.

THE HEAVENLY TWINS. By SARAH GRAND.

IDEALA. By SARAH GRAND.

OUR MANIFOLD NATURE. By SARAH GRAND. With a Portrait of the Author.

THE WHITE TERROR: a Romance of the French Revolution and After. By FELIX GRAS.

THE TERROR; a Romance of the French Revolution. By FÉLIX GRAS.

THE HOUSE OF HIDDEN TREASURE. By MAXWELL GRAY.

THE LAST SENTENCE. By MAXWELL GRAY, Author of "The Silence of Dean Maitland," &c.

THE FREEDOM OF HENRY MEREDYTH. By M. HAMILTON.

McLEOD OF THE CAMERONS. By M. HAMILTON.

A SELF-DENYING ORDINANCE. By M. HAMILTON.

𝔉iction.—𝔓opular 6s. 𝔑ovels.

THE SLAVE. By ROBERT HICHENS.

THE LONDONERS: An Absurdity. By ROBERT HICHENS.

FLAMES. By ROBERT HICHENS.

THE FOLLY OF EUSTACE. By ROBERT HICHENS.

AN IMAGINATIVE MAN. By ROBERT HICHENS.

THE VALLEY OF THE GREAT SHADOW. By ANNIE E. HOLDSWORTH.

THE GODS ARRIVE. By ANNIE E. HOLDSWORTH.

THE YEARS THAT THE LOCUST HATH EATEN. By ANNIE E. HOLDSWORTH.

A BATTLE AND A BOY. By BLANCHE WILLIS HOWARD. With Thirty-nine Illustrations by A. MAC-NIELL-BARBOUR.

THE TWO MAGICS. By HENRY JAMES.

WHAT MAISIE KNEW. By HENRY JAMES.

THE OTHER HOUSE. By HENRY JAMES.

THE SPOILS OF POYNTON. By HENRY JAMES.

EMBARRASSMENTS. By HENRY JAMES.

TERMINATIONS. By HENRY JAMES.

THE AWKWARD AGE. By HENRY JAMES.

ON THE EDGE OF THE EMPIRE. By EDGAR JEPSON and CAPTAIN D. BEAMES.

HERBERT VANLENNERT. By C. F. KEARY.

THE NAULAHKA. A Tale of West and East. By RUDYARD KIPLING and WOLCOTT BALESTIER.

IN HASTE AND AT LEISURE. By Mrs. LYNN LINTON, Author of "Joshua Davidson," &c.

AT THE GATE OF SAMARIA. By W. J. LOCKE.

RELICS. Fragments of a Life. By FRANCES MACNAB.

LIFE AT TWENTY. By CHARLES RUSSELL MORSE.

THE DRONES MUST DIE. By MAX NORDAU.

THE MALADY OF THE CENTURY. By MAX NORDAU.

A COMEDY OF SENTIMENT. By MAX NORDAU.

MARIETTA'S MARRIAGE. By W. E. NORRIS.

THE DANCER IN YELLOW. By W. E. NORRIS.

A VICTIM OF GOOD LUCK. By W. E. NORRIS.

Fiction.—Popular 6s. Novels.

RED ROCK. By Thomas Nelson Page. Illustrated.

EZEKIEL'S SIN. By J. H. Pearce.

A PASTORAL PLAYED OUT. By M. L. Pendered.

AS IN A LOOKING GLASS. By F. C. Philips. With Illustrations by Du Maurier.

THE SCOURGE-STICK. By Mrs. Campbell Praed.

WITHOUT SIN. By Martin J. Pritchard.

KING CIRCUMSTANCE. By Edwin Pugh.

THE MAN OF STRAW. By Elwin Pugh.

TONY DRUM. A Cockney Boy. By Edwin Pugh. With Ten full-page Illustrations by the Beggarstaff Brothers.

THE CAPTAIN OF THE PARISH. By John Quine.

CHUN-TI-KUNG. By Claude Rees.

BELOW THE SALT. By Elizabeth Robins (C. E. Raimond).

THE OPEN QUESTION. By Elizabeth Robins.

CHIMÆRA. By F. Mabel Robinson.

THE DULL MISS ARCHINARD. By Anne Douglas Sedgwick.

THE CONFOUNDING OF CAMELIA. By Anne Douglas Sedgwick.

THE FAILURE OF SIBYL FLETCHER. By Adeline Sergeant.

OUT OF DUE SEASON. By Adeline Sergeant.

THE RAPIN. By H. de Vere Stacpoole.

ON THE FACE OF THE WATERS. By Flora Annie Steel.

THE POTTER'S THUMB. By Flora Annie Steel.

FROM THE FIVE RIVERS. By Flora Annie Steel.

IN THE PERMANENT WAY. By Flora Annie Steel.

THE MINISTER OF STATE. By J. A. Steuart.

Fiction.—Popular 6s. Novels.

THE ELEVENTH COMMANDMENT. By HALLIWELL SUTCLIFFE.

A COURT INTRIGUE. By BASIL THOMSON.

VIA LUCIS. By KASSANDRA VIVARIA.

THE GADFLY. By E. L. VOYNICH.

THE WAR OF THE WORLDS. By H. G. WELLS.

THE ISLAND OF DOCTOR MOREAU. By H. G. WELLS.

ANDREA. By PERCY WHITE.

CORRUPTION. By PERCY WHITE.

MR. BAILEY-MARTIN. By PERCY WHITE. With Portrait.

THEY THAT WALK IN DARKNESS. By I. ZANGWILL.

THE MASTER. By I. ZANGWILL. With Portrait.

CHILDREN OF THE GHETTO. By I. ZANGWILL.

THE PREMIER AND THE PAINTER. A Fantastic Romance. By I. ZANGWILL and LOUIS COWEN.

DREAMERS OF THE GHETTO. By I. ZANGWILL.

THE KING OF SCHNORRERS, GROTESQUES AND FANTASIES. By I. ZANGWILL. With Ninety-eight Illustrations.

THE CELIBATES' CLUB. By I. ZANGWILL.

CLEO THE MAGNIFICENT. By Z. Z.

THE WORLD AND A MAN. By Z. Z.

A DRAMA IN DUTCH. By Z. Z.

Popular 5s. Novels.

THE SECRET OF NARCISSE. By EDMUND GOSSE. Crown 8vo, buckram.

VANITAS. By VERNON LEE, Author of "Hauntings," &c. Crown 8vo, cloth.

THE ATTACK ON THE MILL. By ÉMILE ZOLA. With

Fiction.—Popular 3s. 6d. Novels.

MAMMON. A Novel. By Mrs. ALEXANDER.

LOS CERRITOS. A Romance of the Modern Time. By GERTRUDE FRANKLIN ATHERTON.

THE AVERAGE WOMAN. By WOLCOTT BALESTIER. With an Introduction by HENRY JAMES.

THE JUSTIFICATION OF ANDREW LEBRUN. By F. BARRETT.

PERCHANCE TO DREAM, and other Stories. By MARGARET S. BRISCOE.

CAPT'N DAVY'S HONEYMOON, The Blind Mother, and The Last Confession. By HALL CAINE.

A MARKED MAN: Some Episodes in his Life. By ADA CAMBRIDGE.

A LITTLE MINX. By ADA CAMBRIDGE.

A CONSPIRACY OF SILENCE. By G. COLMORE.

A DAUGHTER OF MUSIC. By G. COLMORE.

BLESSED ARE THE POOR. By FRANÇOIS COPPÉE. With an Introduction by T. P. O'CONNOR.

WRECKAGE, and other Stories. By HUBERT CRACKANTHORPE.

THE KING'S JACKAL. By RICHARD HARDING DAVIES. With Four Illustrations by CHARLES DANA GIBSON.

IN SUMMER ISLES. By BURTON DIBBS.

A COMEDY OF MASKS. By ERNEST DOWSON and ARTHUR MOORE.

THE OUTSPAN. Tales of South Africa. By J. PERCY FITZPATRICK.

A PINCHBECK GODDESS. By Mrs. FLEMING (ALICE M. KIPLING).

THE COPPERHEAD; and other Stories of the North during the American War. By HAROLD FREDERIC.

THE RETURN OF THE O'MAHONY. By HAROLD FREDERIC. With Illustrations.

IN THE VALLEY. By HAROLD FREDERIC. With Illustrations.

Fiction.—Popular 3s. 6d. Novels.

MADEMOISELLE MISS, and other Stories. By HENRY HARLAND.

THE RECIPE FOR DIAMONDS. By C. J. CUTCLIFFE HYNE.

APPASSIONATA: A Musician's Story. By ELSA D'ESTERRE KEELING.

IN THE DWELLINGS OF SILENCE. A Romance of Russia. By WALKER KENNEDY.

A MARRIAGE IN CHINA. By MRS. ARCHIBALD LITTLE.

WRECKERS AND METHODISTS. Cornish Stories. By H. D. LOWRY.

A QUESTION OF TASTE. By MAARTEN MAARTENS.

HER OWN FOLK (En Famille.) By HECTOR MALOT, Author of "No Relations." Translated by Lady MARY LOYD.

A ROMANCE OF THE CAPE FRONTIER. By BERTRAM MITIORD.

'TWEEN SNOW AND FIRE. A Tale of the Kafir War of 1877. By BERTRAM MITFORD.

ELI'S DAUGHTER. By J. II. PEARCE.

INCONSEQUENT LIVES. A Village Chronicle. By J. H. PEARCE.

THE MASTER OF THE MAGICIANS. By ELIZABETH STUART PHELPS and HERBERT D. WARD.

ACCORDING TO ST. JOHN. By AMÉLIE RIVES.

THE STORY OF A PENITENT SOUL. Being the Private Papers of Mr. Stephen Dart, late Minister at Lynnbridge, in the County of Lincoln. By ADELINE SERGEANT.

A KNIGHT OF THE WHITE FEATHER. By TASMA.

UNCLE PIPER OF PIPER'S HILL. By TASMA.

HER LADYSHIP'S ELEPHANT. By DAVID DWIGHT WELLS.

AVENGED ON SOCIETY. By II. F. WOOD.

STORIES FOR NINON. By ÉMILE ZOLA. With a Portrait by WILL ROTHENSTEIN.

Fiction.—Heinemann's International Library

Each Volume has an Introduction specially written by the Editor
Mr. EDMUND GOSSE.

Cloth, 3s. 6d. ; Paper Covers, 2s. 6d.

IN GOD'S WAY. From the Norwegian of BJÖRNSTJERNE BJÖRNSON.

THE HERITAGE OF THE KURTS. From the Norwegian of BJÖRNSTJERNE BJÖRNSON.

FOOTSTEPS OF FATE. From the Dutch of LOUIS COUPERUS.

WOMAN'S FOLLY. From the Italian of GEMMA FERRUGGIA.

THE CHIEF JUSTICE. From the German of KARL EMIL FRANZOS, Author of "For the Right," &c.

THE OLD ADAM AND THE NEW EVE. From the German of RUDOLF GOLM.

A COMMON STORY. From the Russian of IVAN GONT-CHAROFF.

SIREN VOICES (NIELS LYHNE). From the Danish of J. P. JACOBSEN.

THE JEW. From the Polish of JOSEPH IGNATIUS KRASZEWSKI.

THE COMMODORE'S DAUGHTERS. From the Norwegian of JONAS LIE.

NIOBE. From the Norwegian of JONAS LIE.

PIERRE AND JEAN. From the French of GUY DE MAUPASSANT.

FROTH. From the Spanish of Don ARMANDO PALACIO-VALDÉS.

FAREWELL LOVE! From the Italian of MATILDE SERAO.

FANTASY. From the Italian of MATILDE SERAO.

WORK WHILE YE HAVE THE LIGHT. From the Russian of Count LEO TOLSTOY.

PEPITA JIMÉNEZ. From the Spanish of JUAN VALERA.

DOÑA LUZ. From the Spanish of JUAN VALERA.

Fiction.—The Pioneer Series.

Cloth, 3s. net.; Paper Covers, 2s. 6d. net.

The Athenæum.—" If this series keeps up to the present high level of interest, novel readers will have fresh cause for gratitude to Mr. Heinemann."

The Daily Telegraph.—" Mr. Heinemann's genial nursery of up-to-date romance."

The Observer.—" The smart Pioneer Series."

The Manchester Courier.—" The Pioneer Series promises to be as original as many other of Mr. Heinemann's ventures."

The Glasgow Herald.—" This very clever series."

The Sheffield Telegraph.—" The refreshingly original Pioneer Series "

Black and White.—" The brilliant Pioneer Series."

The Liverpool Mercury.—" Each succeeding issue of the Pioneer Series has a character of its own and a special attractiveness."

PAPIER MACHE. By CHARLES ALLEN.

THE NEW VIRTUE. By Mrs. OSCAR BERINGER.

YEKL. A Tale of the New York Ghetto. By A. CAHAN.

LOVE FOR A KEY. By G. COLMORE.

HER OWN DEVICES. By C. G. COMPTON.

MILLY'S STORY. By Mrs. MONTAGUE CRACKANTHORPE.

THE RED BADGE OF COURAGE. By STEPHEN CRANE.

THE LITTLE REGIMENT. By STEPHEN CRANE.

A MAN WITH A MAID. By Mrs. HENRY DUDENEY.

LITTLE BOB. By GYP.

ACROSS AN ULSTER BOG. By M. HAMILTON.

THE GREEN CARNATION. By ROBERT HICHENS.

JOANNA TRAILL, SPINSTER. By ANNIE E. HOLDS-WORTH.

THE DEMAGOGUE AND LADY PHAYRE. By WILLIAM J. LOCKE.

MRS. MUSGRAVE — AND HER HUSBAND. By RICHARD MARSH.

AN ALTAR OF EARTH. By THYMOL MONK.

A STREET IN SUBURBIA. By E. W. PUGH.

THE NEW MOON. By ELIZABETH ROBINS (C. E. RAIMOND).

GEORGE MANDEVILLE'S HUSBAND. By ELIZABETH ROBINS (C. E. RAIMOND).

DARTNELL: A Bizarre Incident. By BENJAMIN SWIFT.

THE WINGS OF ICARUS. By LAURENCE ALMA-TADEMA.

ONE OF GOD'S DILEMMAS. By ALLEN UPWARD.

𝔉iction.—𝔓rice 3s. net.

LITTLE JOHANNES. By F. Van Eeden. Translated from
the Dutch by Clara Bell. With an Introduction by Andrew Lang.
16mo, cloth, silver top, 3s. net.

THE NOVELS OF BJÖRNSTJERNE BJÖRNSON.
Uniform Edition. Edited by Edmund Gosse. Fcap. 8vo, cloth, 3s. net.
each volume.

I. **SYNNÖVÉ SOLBAKKEN.** With Introductory
Essay by Edmund Gosse, and a Portrait of the Author.
II. **ARNE.**
III. **A HAPPY BOY.**
IV. **THE FISHER LASS.**
V. **THE BRIDAL MARCH, AND A DAY.**
VI. **MAGNHILD, AND DUST.**
VII. **CAPTAIN MANSANA, AND MOTHER'S
HANDS.**
VIII. **ABSALOM'S HAIR, AND A PAINFUL
MEMORY.**

THE NOVELS OF IVAN TURGENEV. Uniform Edi-
tion. Translated by Constance Garnett. Fcap. 8vo, cloth, 3s. net.
each volume, or The Set of 15 Volumes £2 2s. net.

The Athenæum.—"Mrs. Garnett deserves the heartiest thanks of her country-
men and countrywomen for putting before them in an English dress the splendid
creations of the great Russian novelist. Her versions are both faithful and
spirited : we have tested them many times."

I. **RUDIN.** With a Portrait of the Author and an
Introduction by Stepniak.
II. **A HOUSE OF GENTLEFOLK.**
III. **ON THE EVE.**
IV. **FATHERS AND CHILDREN.**
V. **SMOKE.**
VI., VII. **VIRGIN SOIL.**
VIII., IX. **A SPORTSMAN'S SKETCHES.**
X. **DREAM TALES AND PROSE POEMS.**
XI. **THE TORRENTS OF SPRING, &c.**
XII. **A LEAR OF THE STEPPES, &c.**
XIII. **THE DIARY OF A SUPERFLUOUS MAN, &c.**
XIV. **A DESPERATE CHARACTER, &c.**
XV. **THE JEW, &c.**

𝔓opular 2s. 6d. 𝔑ovels.

THE CHRISTIAN. By Hall Caine. Paper covers.
THE DOMINANT SEVENTH :—A Musical Story. By
Kate Elizabeth Clarke.
THE TIME MACHINE. By H. G. Wells.
⁎ Also in paper, 1s. 6d.

𝔥einemann's 𝔑ovel 𝔏ibrary.

Price 1s. 6d. net.

THE KING OF THE MOUNTAINS. By EDMOND ABOUT.

KITTY'S FATHER. By FRANK BARRETT.

THE FOURTH NAPOLEON. By CHARLES BENHAM.

COME LIVE WITH ME AND BE MY LOVE. By ROBERT BUCHANAN.

THE THREE MISS KINGS. By ADA CAMBRIDGE.

NOT ALL IN VAIN. By ADA CAMBRIDGE.

MR. BLAKE OF NEWMARKET. By E. H. COOPER.

ORIOLE'S DAUGHTER. By JESSIE FOTHERGILL.

THE TENOR AND THE BOY. By SARAH GRAND.

THE REDS OF THE MIDI. By FELIX GRAS.

NOR WIFE NOR MAID. By MRS. HUNGERFORD.

THE HOYDEN. By MRS. HUNGERFORD.

THE O'CONNORS OF BALLINAHINCH. By MRS. HUNGERFORD.

DAUGHTERS OF MEN. By HANNAH LYNCH.

A ROMANCE OF THE FIRST CONSUL. By MATILDA MALLING.

THE TOWER OF TADDEO. By OUIDA.

THE GRANDEE. By A. PALACIO-VALDÉS.

DONALD MARCY. By ELIZABETH STUART PHELPS.

THE HEAD OF THE FIRM. By MRS. RIDDELL.

LOU. By BARON VON ROBERTS.

THE SURRENDER OF MARGARET BELLARMINE. By ADELINE SERGEANT.

ST. IVES. By ROBERT LOUIS STEVENSON.

THE PENANCE OF PORTIA JAMES. By TASMA.

MISS GRACE OF ALL SOULS. By W. EDWARDS TIREBUCK.

THE NORTH AMERICAN REVIEW.

Edited by GEORGE B. M. HARVEY.

Published monthly.   Price 2s. 6d.

THE BADMINTON MAGAZINE.

Published monthly.   Price 1s.

Lightning Source UK Ltd.
Milton Keynes UK
UKOW05f2339240117

292781UK00001B/70/P

9 781334 490842